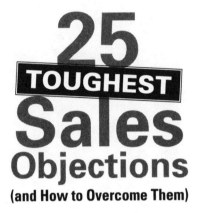

25
TOUGHEST
Sales
Objections
(and How to Overcome Them)

25 TOUGHEST Sales Objections

(and How to Overcome Them)

Surefire Techniques for Conquering Any Resistance and Closing the Deal

Stephan Schiffman

NEW YORK   CHICAGO   SAN FRANCISCO
LISBON   LONDON   MADRID   MEXICO CITY   MILAN
NEW DELHI   SAN JUAN   SEOUL   SINGAPORE
SYDNEY   TORONTO

ISBN: 978-0-07-176737-8
MHID: 0-07-176737-1

e-ISBN: 978-0-07-177344-7
e-MHID: 0-07-177344-4

Interior design by Mauna Eichner and Lee Fukui

This publication is designed to provide accurate and authoritative information in regard to the subject matter covered. It is sold with the understanding that neither the author nor the publisher is engaged in rendering legal, accounting, securities trading, or other professional service. If legal advice or other expert assistance is required, the services of a competent professional person should be sought.

> —*From a Declaration of Principles Jointly Adopted by a Committee of the American Bar Association and a Committee of Publishers and Associations*

McGraw-Hill books are available at special quantity discounts to use as premiums and sales promotions or for use in corporate training programs. To contact a representative, please e-mail us at bulksales@mcgraw-hill.com.

This book is printed on acid-free paper.

To: Justin Eli

CONTENTS

ACKNOWLEDGMENTS

My sincere thanks for the success of this project go to Stephanie, Monika, Gary, Tom Jared, Darren Newton, Anthony Barolo, Toby Heffernan, Josh Sanders and, of course, Anne, Daniele, and Jennifer.

And a special thanks to all the salespeople who work each day to "slay the dragon."

PREFACE:
WHEN IS AN OBJECTION
NOT AN OBJECTION?

In the more than 30 years I've been in sales, I suppose I've heard just about every "objection" there is. And I can tell you that the sign of a real salesperson—someone who's committed to clinching that deal, no matter what—is how he or she deals with these obstacles.

After all, it's a fact of life that in most selling situations we're going to encounter clients who come up with just about every conceivable reason not to buy from us. Sometimes the reasons will sound pretty normal ("I just don't think your product's right for us"), sometimes a bit off center ("You remind me of another salesman at another company I worked at, and he didn't work out for me"), and sometimes they don't seem to make any sense at all ("I don't really like to close deals on a Tuesday").

All too often, when salespeople are presented with an objection, they act as if they've walked into a brick wall. They back off, rub their bruises, and turn toward another prospect who seems as if she or he offers fewer problems. What is lost, though, is one of the most basic facts of sales: *an "objection" is only an objection until it becomes an opportunity.*

Perhaps you think I'm blowing smoke, but hear me out. As salespeople, our ability to overcome objections from our clients is basic to our skills. It's all the difference between hitting our targets every month and slowly watching our commissions dwindle away. The mistake we make is not recognizing the difference between a genuine objection and one that's merely a smokescreen, tossed up by the client to avoid closing the sale.

In the following pages we're going to explore together 25 of the biggest and most common "objections" salespeople encounter. We'll look at how and why these come up, what they mean, and what you should say when you encounter them—and trust me, you're *going* to encounter them at some point in the course of your career.

Most important, we'll learn how to recognize a genuine objection, as opposed to an obstacle. The difference is important. An obstacle can be overcome; a genuine objection can't (although we'll also see that there are ways to gain a long-term advantage from an objection).

Before we start, though, let's go over a quick rundown of my basic principles of selling. These have been developed and tested over a long time, and they run throughout all my books. They're at the heart of the strategies for overcoming sales obstacles and turning them into opportunities. So here's the gist of the Schiffman sales philosophy:

1. Every client has a problem, and your object, as a salesperson, is to solve that problem. If the client didn't have a problem, she or he wouldn't be sitting listening to your pitch.

2. To find out what your client's problem is, you have to ask questions. There's no shortcut to doing so. Your client knows a lot more than you do about what her needs are. And the only way to find out what she's thinking is to ask her.

3. You have to listen. Some salespeople let their minds go to another place when the client's talking. They may make an occasional deal, but they'll never hit the big bucks. Some used to say that salespeople had to be smooth talkers. That's not even half of the equation. To be a great salesperson, you've also got to be a great listener.

4. What a client says he wants is not necessarily what he really wants. In fact, a lot of clients don't know what they want. Your job as a salesperson is to help the client solve his problem, *even if he doesn't yet know what problem he wants solved.* (Just to be clear on this, your job is not to solve *your* problem. Your client doesn't care about your problem, which probably has to do with the size of your commission. Never has. Never will.)

5. Every sales discussion has somewhere in it the seeds of a win-win solution. They may be buried very deeply, but if you can find a way to get to them, you can nurture and cultivate them, and they'll blossom and bear fruit.

We'll return again to these five basic points. But for now, you should just read them over carefully, think about them, and see how they apply to your day-to-day practice in the field.

Now let's turn to the objections, starting with this basic question: when is an objection not an objection?

INTRODUCTION:
WHY DO PEOPLE BUY STUFF?

Of all the sales objections you'll encounter, one of the most common is "the price is too high."

You've got a great product. You've assembled a presentation that stresses the product's benefits and its strengths. You're completely confident that that product outstrips anything else in the marketplace. And yet your client says it doesn't fit his budget.

I'll discuss the specifics of overcoming this objection a bit more in Chapter 1. But I am using it here to illustrate something about how and why people make decisions to buy things.

Fundamentally, people buy stuff because that stuff—whether a product or a service—solves a problem. They may not think of it in terms of a problem. The couple who decide to spend 20 bucks to go see a movie Saturday afternoon are probably not thinking, "Gosh, we've got a problem. Let's go see a movie." Rather, they just want to be entertained, and they're willing to put a price on their need for entertainment. (Don't get me started on the cost of entertainment these days; a movie, popcorn, and a couple of sodas are probably around $40.)

When you're selling to a prospect, a lead, or an established client, your central challenge is to determine what value your audience puts on the problem, because cost is contingent on the *value the customer puts on the goods or service.* It's pretty basic capitalism. The more a customer values something, the more he'll pay for it.

Allow me to illustrate with an example from the dog food industry.

I know, I know—this seems a long way away from sales objections—just bear with me.

For a long time the dog food industry segmented its customer base into four basic groups: big dogs, small dogs, young dogs, and old dogs. It seemed like a very sensible, very stable system.

Until someone pointed out, it wasn't the dogs who were buying the dog food.

The manufacturers did a double take. And then they reassessed their customer segmentation studies. They decided to focus not on the dogs, who clearly couldn't influence customer choice, but on the *attitudes of the dog owners toward their dogs.*

They came up with a new segmentation. There were still four groups, but now instead of dogs they were groups of human customers. And they were divided by what they thought of their dogs.

- *Group 1: Dog as Animal.* The dog is an animal that lives either in the house or out of the house and serves a useful function. For example, a farm dog might catch rats, keep predators away from other animals, and serve as a guard for the family. But regarding food, price is an important consideration, because the dog's value is limited (after all, if it dies, you can always get another one).

- *Group 2: Dog as Pet.* The dogs in this group have a stronger emotional tie to the consumer. They're something more than a tool; the customer cares about the dog, but still its importance is mainly functional. We grieve for our pets when they pass away, but not in the same way that we care when a relative dies. So the price of keeping a pet healthy is still important but probably not to quite the degree that we care about keeping ourselves and our loved ones in good shape.

- *Group 3: Dog as Child.* Now we're getting closer to it. Consumers care about these dogs to a much greater degree than the consumers in Groups 1 and 2. And by the same token, they place less stress on the price on the dog food they buy and more emphasis on its healthy qualities. They're more concerned with the balance of vitamins, the proportion of grains, proteins, and so on. The dog has become a member of the family, and they care about it in the same way they'd be concerned about their child's diet.

- *Group 4: Dog as Grandchild.* Nothing's too good for a dog in this category. Price? No object. In the same way that we shamelessly spoil our grandchildren (and I'm speaking here as a grandfather!), dog owners in Group 4 spoil their pooches. Clearly, if a vendor is selling to members of Group 4, she or he can charge the sky as long as the emphasis is on the health-giving benefits of the food. All the force of the sales presentation has to be on the specific advantages of buying this kind of food for health, energy, glossy coat, and so on. Price can be mentioned last, as a kind of afterthought.

I cite this example to show why the objection "it costs too much" has to be viewed in its proper context. *A product only costs too much if the customer believes its value is below its price.* So the first problem you, as a salesperson, have is to figure out what the customer values about the product.

This leads me to the second point. Why do people buy stuff?

It's simple. *People buy things that solve their problems.* This is a basic truth that's often lost. If someone wants to be entertained, she buys something that entertains her. If she needs a product to complete part of her job, she buys whatever will do that.

So part of your challenge with this objection is to put a dollar quantity on the problem the product solves. Sometimes this is comparatively easy. You can use the customers' numbers—which you've researched and studied—to calculate the customers' savings if they buy your product, as opposed to your competition. You also need to find a bottom-dollar amount—the price you need to charge to make your profit margin while at the same time meeting the customers' idea of the value of their problem.

At that point, your challenge becomes convincing customers of the validity of your conclusion. And that can take some work.

Step One: Take them through the numbers. You should have these at the tip of your tongue. Know the costs they're incurring, the prices your competitors are charging, and the savings the customers will reap if they purchase your product to solve their problem. The most important thing you need to know is how much their current problem is costing them. That's what they are willing to pay.

Step Two: Don't let yourself be pushed away. A while ago, I was running a sales seminar and a woman told the group that she'd recently faced a price objection. The customer told her he wasn't going to pay her price, and that was that.

But she persisted. She said she was going to try again. "You never know," she said. "You never know when something you say will change his mind. Maybe I won't even know what it is when I say it."

I thought: that's very much to the point. Because a big part of sales success is not letting the customer's objection defeat you.

You've got to keep trying, keep developing different arguments, and, most important *keep asking questions*. And sooner or later you'll get through and make the sale.

Step Three: Figure out what's behind the objection. Price is an easy objection for customers to make because it's something that occurs to them first. It's always possible for customers to say (and to think) that they're paying too much. But in many cases, that's really not what the objection's about, it's just what they're saying it's about. So you need to determine if your price is *really* too high or whether there's something else involved (in which case, you need to move on to the appropriate chapter of this book).

Step Four: Don't overreact. This is a common phenomenon, sometimes born of inexperience on the part of the salesperson and sometimes of sheer desperation or frustration. Let me give you an example.

A salesman I know was sitting in a room making his pitch to the head of a small company. When he'd finished the carefully crafted, PowerPoint-assisted speech that he'd spent weeks on, he sat back and waited for the miracle to happen. He envisioned the CEO telling him it was the best presentation he'd ever heard and of course they'd pick up his product at the asking price. He even thought, so brilliant had been the presentation that the company might bump up its order by a couple of thousand units.

And instead? You guessed it. The CEO sat back, folded his hands across his well-pressed shirt, and said, "I'm sorry. The price is beyond my range. Thanks for coming in."

The salesman—well, okay, I'll admit it was me, but that was a long time ago—immediately got up and said, "I'm sorry, but if you don't understand the value that I'm offering you, I don't think we've got anything more to talk about." I walked out of the room, didn't look back, and completely missed a chance to nail a sale. Because I didn't recognize that what the CEO said was just the first gun in an opening exchange. I should have been mature enough and calm enough to understand that this was only the beginning of a dialogue. Instead, all I could focus on was the work and effort I'd gone to compiling those slides.

Now let's look at these three subobjections from a different perspective: from the point of view of the *customer*. That is, let's figure out what the customer wanted from each part of the objection.

To do this, we're going to have to break our customer down into types—kind of what the dog food industry did in the industry segmentation study that I mentioned previously. There are all kinds of ways we could segment our target customer: by experience and/or corporate title, by age, by sex, and so on. As it happens, for the purposes of this book we'll segment our customers into four basic categories according to their *attitude*:

1. *Dominant.* Customers in this buying style are fast-paced, outspoken, questioning, and skeptical. You can't get anything by them. They'll push you on everything you say, demand that you back it all up, and not accept a single thing on faith. Generally, they're the ones who won't let your presentation go by without interrupting you every few minutes with a comment, query, or complaint.

2. *Influence.* These people are also fast-paced and outspoken, but they're warm and accepting. They're the kind of people we think of as networkers—always anxious to connect with you on as many levels as possible. They want to be your friend, to find out all about you. Questions from them come thick and fast, as they do from Dominants. But

whereas Dominants are about challenging you, Influence customers want to find out all about what makes you tick.

3. *Steadiness.* These customers are warm and accepting, but they're also cautious and reflective. They're far less assertive than the previous two groups. Instead, they want your approval. They want to be absolutely sure that the decision they're making is the right one, and for this reason they can drive you crazy with their inability to actually *make a decision.*

4. *Conscientious.* Finally, there's the group who are cautious and reflective, but at the same time they're questioning and skeptical, just like Group 1. They think about everything, and no matter what you do, you can't get them to be enthusiastic. They take copious notes during your presentation, and they want as much hard data as possible, even when it doesn't exist.

Your first and most important job as a salesperson is to determine what kind of customers you're dealing with. Are they from Group 1, Group 2, Group 3, or Group 4? The best way of finding out, of course, is to ask questions and to listen carefully to the answers. Once you've decided *who* your customers are, you can figure out *what* their objections are.

With this in mind, let's look at the four steps again.

Step One: Take them through the numbers. This will be most important if your customers are part of Group 1 or Group 4. These are the people who will be most skeptical, and for that reason they will want facts to back up your assertions about the product or service. You can't, of course, rely solely on the numbers, but you'll find that your numbers and facts will have the most influence with Groups 1 and 4. Once you convince them that there really is a solid empirical basis for your contention, some of their other questions will resolve themselves.

Don't worry if Group 4 customers don't react right away to your information. They're absorbing it. In the same spirit, Group 1 customers may initially argue with your facts, apparently not wanting to accept them. But if your information is solid, they'll come around in the end.

Step Two: Don't let yourself be pushed away. This is a particularly important step with Groups 1 and 3. It's all too easy to let yourself feel defeated by either of these two customer types. Rather than give up, you need to find a way to come back at them in a meaningful way.

Group 1 is the most aggressive type of customer. People who are part of this group are going to push hard against you. But at the same time, they respect pushback. Because they themselves are strong, they react well to strength.

Several years ago I ran into a customer who might have been the poster child for this type. He was a large guy, towering over me (full disclosure—I'm not that tall), and had perfected the art of looming over salespeople, even when he was sitting down. As I started my presentation, he leaned forward in his chair, lowered his head, and glowered at me from under a pair of beetle brows. His voice came in a low, feral growl.

"That's *not* what I need," he snarled. "The cost is *way* above my budget. No *way* am I paying that much!"

I could feel sweat pricking the back hairs on my neck. If this guy stood up, he could intimidate Shaquille O'Neal. But I gathered my courage and said, "Sir, if you sit down and let me finish, I think I can persuade you that my services are worth their price."

He snarled again.

Now I was ticked. I didn't raise my voice; instead, I lowered it to something just above a whisper. "*I will not be interrupted when I'm presenting!*" I said. Hissed, actually.

He sank back in his chair. The entire room relaxed. And I continued with the presentation and wound up making a sale—though I had to send my shoes to the dry cleaner afterward to get rid of the sweat stains in them.

Group 4 type customers can be even more frustrating. Talking to them sometimes feels like you're speaking to a wet carpet. They absorb every bit of energy that comes near them. Nonetheless, you have to persist because, in the back of their minds, they *want* to be persuaded. They just want to make sure they've got all the information they need to make the decision. Patiently, carefully, you need to lead them around their tendency to second-guess themselves and get to a point where not only have they decided to buy your product but they're even happy about it.

Step Three: Figure out what's behind the objection. This is clearly important for all four groups, but it's especially significant for Groups 2 and 3.

Group 2 is apt to mask their objections with friendliness. They don't really like to disagree; it runs against their nature. Instead, they smother you with conversations about anything other than what you want to talk about. Their rejection of your offer is softened by a gentle fall of words, rather like a snowfall, softening the ugly outlines of what they're really saying.

Pleasant as it is to be nicely rejected, rejection is still, well, rejection. And you can't let the matter rest there. Group 2 is the one you've got to push hardest to find out what's behind their problem with your offer. Is it *really* the price? Or is it something much more significant?

Group 3 is, in some respects, a modified version of Group 2. They don't like to reject you, especially not over price. But they just don't want to . . . they just *can't* . . . darn it, they just don't feel they *can!* . . . And so you're left in limbo.

Being pushed away by this group is the ultimate in passive aggression. And you can't let it set you back. Instead, you've got to lead them through the terms of their objections. It isn't going to be easy, because this is a very uncomfortable place for them, but it's essential that you know precisely what they're objecting to. Is it really the price? Is the price really going to bust their budget? Or is it something else entirely?

Step 4: Don't overreact. Again, I might say that this applies to all four groups. But it's especially important for Groups 1 and 2.

For Group 1, the point is pretty obvious. They're aggressive and pushy, so if you overreact, it closes off the conversation, and you're done.

For Group 2, the point is that overreacting negatively goes against their psychological grain. They want to increase their connection with you, and you're pushing them away, irritated by their failure to see what a great deal you're offering them. They can react by becoming sulky or negative, and then you've lost the opportunity to connect with them.

It so happens I have a good friend who's a classic Group 2 type. He's all about forming connections and probably has a list of Facebook friends that's bigger than the New York metropolitan area. But the one thing that really sets him off is if anyone goes negative on him. He hates—I mean *hates*—that, and he'll never listen to another word that person says. If I were selling to him and he raised the price objection, the last thing I'd want to do is turn my back and walk away. Because there's no way I could ever reestablish that contact again.

In this introduction I've established the most important elements of this book: that customers are all different and you have to adapt your selling style to fit these different types. In subsequent chapters we'll return a number of times to the four types of customers. And we'll see how with each type of objection, understanding and absorbing the four types of customers allows us to overcome these objections and clinch the sale.

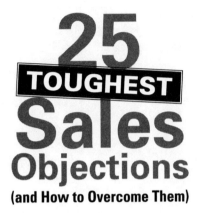

25
TOUGHEST
Sales
Objections
(and How to Overcome Them)

GIVE ME A
BETTER PRICE

In the introduction, I talked a bit about the price objection. Now we're ready for a more detailed discussion. I'm putting this chapter first in the book because it's among the most common objections you'll run into.

For the most part, overcoming this one is a matter of determining what precisely the client *wants*. Some objections are roadblocks. They're intended to stop your discussion in its tracks, and before you can go on, you've got to figure out a way around them or through them. Others, like the one I'll discuss in this chapter, are just bumps in the road. The problem is that sometimes salespeople let them become roadblocks.

Pricing is something that comes up in virtually every sales call, because it's the most obvious point. You should go into the call with the assumption that your lead is not going to want to pay what you're asking and that she or he is going to push back.

THE MISUSE OF DISCOUNTING

Many people think that a negotiation is fundamentally about price. It isn't, of course; that's just one of many factors. But price is the one that springs to most people's minds.

The biggest mistake that salespeople make when confronted with the price objection is to assume that the answer is to discount immediately. It's almost an instinct for some people. And in doing so, they give away far more than they should. For instance, consider the following dialogue:

Client: The price you've named is too high.

Salesperson: Okay, how about if we talk about a 10 percent discount? In fact, we could probably do a bit better than that if you need us to.

Client: [says nothing]

Salesperson: Well, I recognize that this is a bit high, and you're a favored customer. So we could do a 15 percent discount. Would that work?

Client: [says nothing]

Salesperson: All right. I'll go back to my boss and see if we can commit to a 20 percent discount. How does that sound?

Client: Fine.

There are several things to take note of in this exchange:

1. The client, by saying almost nothing, has gotten a discount of at least 15 percent and quite possibly 20 percent.

2. The proportion of talking between client and salesperson is skewed the wrong way. The salesperson is doing about 80 percent of the *talking* instead of 80 percent of the *listening*.

3. The salesperson assumes that price is the only thing that matters to the client.

4. The salesperson assumes that the only leverage he has is to discount.

5. The client hasn't had to give up anything to get the discount. In fact, she hasn't been asked for anything. The salesperson is so anxious to land the sale that he's discounting as a strategy.

This is the biggest error in this scenario: *discounting isn't a strategy.* It's a tactic—something that should be done to achieve a particular end. In this case, discounting is legitimate if it leads to the client making concessions in some other part of the sale. Otherwise, it's just giving away money.

Several years ago, I was training for a corporation. After watching a group of its salespeople make cold calls for a morning, I called a meeting of the executives. "Do you realize," I said, "that all your salespeople are routinely discounting 10 to 20 percent?"

Silence.

"Why are you giving away 20 percent at the start of the call?"

Silence.

Everyone looked sheepish, and then someone from the back of the room piped up with, "Well, even with a 20 percent discount, they're still making the sales."

"Sure," I replied. "But you're leaving money on the table. In fact, you're not just leaving it on the table, you're pushing it over to the client and asking him to take it away from you. Why would you *do* that?"

No one could give me a good answer. And I began to realize that for them, the act of making the sale was more important than the content of the sale itself. That is an attitude that in the long run is going to lose a company money.

By not focusing on the terms of the sale but instead simply discounting in order to persuade the lead to buy, the salesperson is giving up things that he doesn't need to and creating an atmosphere in which he can't help but lose to the client. Moreover, doing so sets a dangerous precedent—the next time he comes back to make another pitch, the client will expect an automatic discount. To make his new offer attractive, the salesperson will have to discount even more than the previous time. And so the vicious cycle goes on until the salesperson realizes that his commission has disappeared with a loud "pop!"

The salesperson in this instance assumed that the client only cared about price, so logically (from his point of view), the only strategy to counter this objection was to start discounting. In fact, price is one of a large number of factors that matter to the client. Ironically, it's the one most removed from the salesperson's control. After all, as a member of the sales staff you don't set the product's price. That's done by executives who are concerned about the company's bottom line. So when you come to negotiate price, you're dealing with something in which you don't have a big stake. Not only that, you may not even know all the considerations that went into determining that price.

What You Should Keep in Mind about Price

Going into a sales call, here are the main things you should know about the price of your product or service:

1. How does it compare to similar products or services offered throughout the industry?

2. What was the last price your client paid for this product or service?

3. Was that price set by your company or by a competitor?

4. Has the price for this product or service been rising or falling?

5. What are the consequences to the client if you can't clinch the sale?

Knowledge of these points will help you know how genuine the objection is and how hard you can push back against it.

WHAT'S IT REALLY ABOUT?

Another big mistake of our salesperson in the previous scenario was to assume that because the client raised the point about price, that is really the central problem the client is concerned about.

Sometimes the objection is clearly about price. But other times it's a factor that conceals another aspect of the product that the client doesn't want to talk about. The salesperson has to find a lever to push open the door and see what's behind it.

For example:

Client: I appreciate your comments, and I'm impressed with what you've shown me, but I have to tell you that unit price is a big issue for us.

Salesperson: I see. Would you give me an idea of the kind of range you had in mind?

Client: Well, we were thinking of something between 40 cents and 42 cents a unit, but . . .

Salesperson: That's certainly a point for discussion.

Client: To tell you the truth, I'm not sure that even at that price the product would be the right one for us.

Salesperson: Would you explain?

Client: What we're looking for is something that has a more flexible range of functions. Of course, that would mean an increased price, and I know that that puts it out of range with your product.

Salesperson: I see. So what you're looking for is a product that can do more but isn't a lot more expensive?

Client: Yes. That's it.

Salesperson: Well, I think we can discuss that. Of course, increasing functionality will add to production time, so we may not be able to supply as many units in the time frame that you indicated.

Client: Well, we've got some flexibility with delivery.

As you can see from this dialogue, price wasn't really the objection. It was part of the problem—because the client assumed that more features meant a higher price. But as we've seen several times already, that's not always the case. What you can show clients is that a lower price can be traded off for something that's less important to them.

What Does the Client Need?

In 1943 the psychologist Abraham Maslow published a paper in which he said that humans have what he termed "a hierarchy of needs." This hierarchy is like a pyramid. The broadest needs on the bottom of the pyramid have to be met before humans can move on to satisfy those higher up on the pyramid.

I don't agree in full with Maslow—not necessarily much at all—but there's a point to this idea of a hierarchy of needs that's useful for salespeople.

Clients have needs because they have problems that must be solved. But not all these needs are equal. Some are more important than others. When you first meet with clients, you need to spend some time deciding what their needs are and then giving them an order. Start by working on the big problems first and then gradually ascend through the pyramid to the smaller, less important needs. At the end, you'll have very satisfied—in Maslow's terminology, "self-actualized"—clients.

Price, because it's a big topic, often winds up toward the base of client needs. Once you get past it, you can start thinking about other things. But pricing has to be resolved first.

IF THE PRICE CAN'T BE CUT

As mentioned, discounting is a tactic. It can be used judiciously to get the client to concede on other questions—delivery date, features, and so on. But there may come a point when you can't make the price any lower than it is.

At that point, it's time to take out more tricks from your bag. If the price can't be cut, what can you offer? Speeded-up delivery? A discount on shipping? An extended service warranty?

Just keep in mind that for every one of these concessions, you need to look for something in return from the client.

Where to Start

Before starting any discussion about price, there's one more thing you need to know: the number you can't go below. Clearly the number you propose is going to be substantially above this amount, because you need some room to go down. But as you near your bottom number, you need to get more creative with alternatives to dropping the price. You also need to think about the impact each of these other factors will have on your company's bottom line. If you drop the base price but at the same time get the client to make concessions in a service agreement, will this save your company money in the long run?

WHO MAKES THIS OBJECTION?

All four groups will make the price objection, but they will take different approaches. The trick is to figure out the type of person who's raising the objection and react appropriately.

1. *Dominant.* This group is inclined to raise the price objection because they have gotten information that you're outpricing the competition. Or you've jacked the price up since the last time you paid a sales call. Or you're underestimating their ability to guess what you're really up to. In any case, they aren't inclined to take anything you say at face value. Instead, they're going to question everything you say and challenge you at every opportunity. It's infuriating, but you can meet them on their own terms. Challenge their questions. Ask them the source of their information. Back up your pricing with cold, hard data. Facts are what this group respects.

2. *Influence.* This group, because of its networked connections, knows a lot about what's going on in the industry. They know exactly what kinds of pricing are out there, who's paying what for what, and what kind of discounts are

being offered by your competitors. They take the same approach to you. In fact, if you're not cautious, they are apt to wheedle out of you crucial business information that you'd rather keep confidential. You need to be prudent with this group, but at the same time, take advantage of their friendliness to open negotiations on what trade-offs for lower pricing they would consider.

3. *Steadiness.* This group raises the pricing objection in a tentative manner: "Isn't the unit price that you're asking kind of high? Couldn't you consider taking it down a bit? Do you think that's the kind of price that XYZ Corporation is asking?" They're also often inclined to use pricing to mask another underlying objection. The best way to approach them is to be short, factual, and blunt: "No, the price we're offering actually *is* competitive. Yes, I could consider lowering it, but only at the cost of something else. The XYZ Corporation's prices are higher and their product is less reliable. Now, what do you want to do?"

4. *Conscientious.* Pricing for this group isn't necessarily a huge consideration. They're not really excited about anything. Fill them full of statistics and information and don't expect them to have a big reaction to much of anything. You're just not going to get one. But if you can give them enough data, you'll make the sale.

I WANT TO COMPARE PRICES WITH ANOTHER VENDOR

Imagine, for a minute, a hardworking salesperson working through a pitch. He's gathered all the important information on his client, so he knows what points to emphasize and what problems his product will solve. He's being careful to ask a lot of questions and to allow the client to do most of the talking, at least during the first part of the pitch.

He gathers together the threads of his argument and, glancing at his watch to keep an eye on the time, brings all the force of his personality into the last couple of sentences. He finishes with a clear, strong invitation to the client to buy.

There! It's over. Nothing left now but for the client to see the ironclad logic of his presentation. In his mind he's already out the door, in his car, and heading to a restaurant to celebrate the sale with a big lunch before calling the office to report in.

The client taps a pencil against a yellow pad. She glances down through the notes she's made during the presentation and taps again.

Something's clicking in the back of the salesperson's mind. Why isn't she saying anything? She should be naming the size of her order at this point. He leans forward.

"Is there anything else you want to ask?"

She shakes her head. The pencil continues to tap. The salesperson is becoming hypnotized by it. *Tap . . . tap . . . tap . . .*

"Do you need me to run over the delivery schedule again?"

"No, thanks." *Tap . . . tap . . . tap . . .*

"Any questions or concerns about quantities available?"

There's a shake of the head. *Tap . . . tap . . . tap . . .*

Then she stops, looks up, and gives a half smile. "Thanks very much for the presentation. I've got another vendor coming in next week, and I'll have to see what they're offering. I'll let you know."

The salesperson's stomach hits his shoes. He can barely stand up to shake hands; he knows he's sweating. And before he realizes it, he's out the door and in his car, heading . . . well, maybe to a bar instead of a restaurant.

THE DELAYING TACTIC

What's particularly frustrating about this objection is that, to many salespeople, there doesn't seem to be an immediate response to it. After all, what's really wrong with comparison shopping? Shouldn't any conscientious executive check the prices available from different vendors before making an informed and responsible decision?

All true, of course. But the question you've got to ask yourself when you meet this objection is, does the client *really* need the time to do this research and comparison? Or is this a non-objection objection designed to get you out the door and on your way?

Clearly, if you determine that the executive's concern is genuine, it's relatively easy to ensure that your conversation will continue at a later date and that you'll have an opportunity to counter whatever issues your competitors may raise in the client's mind (I'll show you how to do this later).

But equally important, *you must find out if this objection is genuine.* If it turns out that the stated "objection" is no more than a tactic aimed at ending the conversation, you need to make a countermove.

TELLTALE SIGNS

I'm not much of a poker player, although I admit that there have been some very pleasant evenings when friends and I have sat around a green cloth-topped table, piles of chips in front of us and drinks and cigars at the ready. I usually wind up about even after such evenings or sometimes at a slight loss. But even though I'll never be able to win the World Series of Poker at Vegas, I know enough to understand that everyone has certain signs— "tells" in Pokerspeak—that an experienced player can read. At least part of the art of successful poker playing is learning to read these tells in your opponent, to know when she's bluffing on a pair of twos and when she's really holding a straight flush.

Tells are involuntary; for the most part we're not aware we give off these signals. But learning to read them can be as invaluable for a salesperson as for a gambler. They are so because they give you an all-important edge in understanding what your client is thinking and how much or how little she is *really* objecting to what you're saying.

During any sales presentation, you should spend the overwhelming amount of it looking at the client. (I don't mean staring, which can be off-putting and unpleasant, but just looking in a very natural way.) Avoid at all costs reading off note cards or a PowerPoint presentation—at most, glance down at your personal digital assistant (PDA) to refresh your memory about a fact or figure. But mostly you should meet the client's gaze. If there's more than one person you're presenting to, shift your look from one to the other—not rapidly, which leads to "shifty eyes" and makes you look nervous and furtive, but naturally, every 15 or 20 seconds.

While you're doing this, as one part of your brain is concentrating on making the best, most forceful and informative presentation possible, another part should be soaking up details about how the client or clients are reacting—not just in their words but in their body language. Here are some of the things to look for:

- Are they frequently glancing at their watches or a clock in the room?

- Is their attention focused on you, or are they looking at one another?

- Are their arms or legs crossed (an important body language signal that generally indicates resistance to what's being said)?

- Are they making any repetitive movements—tapping pencils, twirling pens, playing with paper clips?

- Are they shifting in their seats and/or clearing their throats more than seems necessary?

Some or all of these things may indicate that your audience is bored, inattentive, or looking for a way out of the room and back to what they think is more important business. If, after observing these signs, you run into an objection, you're probably safe in assuming that the basis of the objection isn't genuine, and you can tailor your response accordingly.

Note that some tells are particular to individuals. It was once written of a certain prominent American politician that you could always tell when he was lying because when he lied, he repeated himself. As you get to know the people you're selling to, you'll begin to detect their individual tells and be able to read them better.

CONTINUING THE CONVERSATION

When this objection is raised, whether it's genuine or not, there's very little point in trying to force an immediate decision. If the customer really wants more information about what the competition is offering in order to make an informed decision, she's going to get annoyed if you try to force her into a hasty commitment, one that could rebound on her career if it goes wrong.

Also, if the client is making the objection just to end your pitch and get you out of the building, you're not helping yourself by planting your feet firmly on the ground and refusing to budge. Such a course will mark you as obstreperous and inflexible, and it's unlikely to help you close a sale. Remember that in this instance, as in all your sales, you're in things for the long haul. You want to maintain a relationship with the client, even if it means putting off a sale until a later date.

The most important thing you want—and I've said this already—is to *continue the conversation.* Just not *right now.*

For this reason, I'd recommend the following steps:

1. *Don't argue; accept that the meeting is over.* Rather than sitting there like a bump on a log, start making the preliminary motions of ending the meeting. Pack up your PowerPoint slides and your samples. You don't need to do so in silence—

it's perfectly okay and advisable to keep talking while you're doing it. (If you don't, you will look sulky.) This action is simply a physical way of acknowledging that the client has ended the meeting and you respect her decision.

2. *Get a commitment for the next meeting.* Say something along the lines of "I completely understand that you want to have all the information before making a decision. Would next Wednesday at 10 a.m. be a good time for us to continue this discussion?" Most likely, at this point the client will refer you to her assistant to set up an appointment. That's fine—as long as you keep your foot in the door.

3. *Stay in touch.* During the interval between the end of this meeting and the beginning of the next, construct a piece of sales material that lays out your product or service next to its most significant competition—including price, delivery time, discounts, functions—and send it to the client. You can introduce it by saying something like, "Hi, _____. Thanks for our meeting yesterday. I thought you might be interested in the following comparisons between my product and X's product. Looking forward to our meeting next Wednesday, when you can ask me further questions about this."

These steps will ensure that your sale is not at an end and that you anticipate the competitors' attempts to sell to your client.

Why don't I recommend bringing up the competition's weaknesses and unfavorable comparisons to what you're selling at the first meeting, when this objection comes up? It's simple. *The client is signaling to you that the meeting is over.* She wants to gather more information; you're not going to preempt that, no matter how well prepared you are to argue your case. In fact, you're much more likely to damage the possibility of a sale by implying that there's something unreasonable about her desire for more information.

In combating this objection, your biggest enemy is your own tendency to hurry. While I understand and sympathize with the need to make a lot of sales in a particular time frame (your company has a budget, you have a quota, and you want your commission), trying to rush some sales is counterproductive. While there are some people who can make a decision to buy instantly, others, whether by temperament or by necessity, take longer. You have to respect that and modify your techniques accordingly.

WHO MAKES THIS OBJECTION?

In trying to determine if the objection of wanting to compare prices with another vendor is genuine, it's crucial that you identify what kind of a person or group of people you're pitching to.

1. *Dominant.* This group loves facts and figures. They like to shoot them at you and watch you dance as you try to react to the barrage of data. It's their way of establishing control of the conversation and, they hope, getting the best deal for their company. Their very desire for data, though, means that they're likely to have done extensive research before meeting you. In all probability, they already know what the competing product costs and all about its relative strengths and weaknesses. For this reason, my feeling is that when Dominant people make this objection it's quite possible that it's a way of trying to end the sale. The counter is to play on their need for facts. Thank them for their time and suggest that when you next meet, you can provide them with some new information about your product that

will, possibly, sway them to purchase it. A profusion of data can help get the sale back on track.

2. *Influence.* The fact that this group is so plugged in means that they're getting information from a variety of sources. Thus, when they tell you that they want more details from the competition, you can be quite sure they mean it. However, your advantage is that they want to stay in touch with you; you're an important part of their network. So you shouldn't have too much trouble setting up the next meeting and continuing to pitch your product or service.

3. *Steadiness.* Of the four groups, this one is most likely to genuinely make this objection. The reason has to do with their reluctance to make decisions. They feel as if they *never* have enough data. Every piece of information raises new questions in their minds. This is one of the things that make them such a frustrating bunch to deal with. However, that same feature makes it doubly important that you send them additional information about what you're selling and how it stacks up against the competition. They'll welcome material such as that with open arms.

4. *Conscientious.* Strictly from the standpoint of tells, this group can be hard to read (that's true of Dominants, as well). Their very lack of emotion in business matters means they're restricted in what signals they send. But they also thirst for data, so if they tell you that they want to compare what you're selling with the product of the competition, don't take it in the wrong spirit if they do it with a gloomy countenance and a limp handshake to close out the meeting. Just follow up with more data and a firm commitment to a future meeting.

I DON'T NEED THE PRODUCT OR SERVICE

One of the cornerstones of my selling system is the proposition that when the client talks, *you've got to listen*. And I mean *really* listen.

Several years ago, I ran a training workshop for salespeople at a midsized company. As part of my research into how the company's salespeople were performing, I listened in on a number of their calls. Some of these calls were made to existing clients, some were attempts to turn prospects into leads, and some were cold calls, looking for prospects.

In all these different types of calls, one thing that struck me was the large percentage of salespeople who weren't taking the trouble to listen. Even when the person on the other end of the phone was talking, I could almost hear the salesperson giving half an ear while running over numbers and arguments in his head. Fingers were drumming, pencils tapping. In one particularly horrendous case, while the client talked, explaining her concerns in detail, the salesperson was checking his BlackBerry! Needless to say, he got a talking-to from me afterward about the first commandment of selling: *the client comes before everything!*

Of course, some of the calls I listened to were successful. Almost any salesperson who makes a large volume of calls, even if they're mediocre, is going to experience some level of success based on the sheer numbers. But this isn't the best, most efficient way to sell.

When the objection that's the subject of this chapter—"I don't need the product or service"—comes up, it's particularly important to listen to the client. The first words out of your mouth after hearing this objection should be, "Would you explain to me why not?"

LISTEN TO THE REASONS

The client, assuming that the objection is genuine on his part and not merely a negotiating technique, will list some reasons why he doesn't think your product or service is needed. It's going to come down to the issue of a problem, because when all is said and done, whatever you're selling has to prevent or solve a problem for the client. So there are three basic reasons why he might think that he doesn't need what you're selling:

1. The problem that it's designed to solve doesn't exist anymore.

2. The problem has grown in scope beyond the ability of your product or service to solve it.

3. The company doesn't think your product or service is really capable of solving the problem.

Let's address each of these reasons in kind.

The Problem No Longer Exists

It occasionally happens that the company has moved on from whatever your product is designed to do and no longer needs it. That is both a disappointment and an opportunity: the former because you're not going to sell the product; the latter because it gives you a chance to evaluate the business anew and discuss with the client what else you can sell him that he *does* need. Your conversation might start something like this:

> *Client:* I'm sorry, but we don't need those widgets anymore.
>
> *Salesperson:* Would you tell me why?
>
> *Client:* Well, we no longer manufacture widget-winders, so your product wouldn't be of any use to us.
>
> *Salesperson:* That's good to know. I'll make a note of that. But let's talk about what sort of widget-winder supplies I might be able to help you with.

The Problem's Too Big

The challenge here is to adjust the client's perception and expectations. If the demand for your product has substantially increased, that's a great chance for you to discuss how to fulfill it. Again, you have to listen. Your conversation might go like this:

> *Client:* I'm sorry, but we don't need those widgets anymore.
>
> *Salesperson:* Would you tell me why?
>
> *Client:* Well, the fact is that our new widget-winders are proving more popular than we thought, and we're taking in

increased supplies of widgets to meet the demand. I just think we've moved to a point beyond the capacity of your company to supply us.

Salesperson: I'm glad to hear you're having such success with your product. I think it's possible we may be able to step up supply, though we'll have to discuss staggering deliveries to accommodate a more aggressive production schedule. How many units are we talking here?

The Client Doesn't Think Your Product or Service Can Solve the Problem

As you build up a client list, you're going to spend many hours with these people. Sometimes salespeople can get blasé about these meetings and think, "Well, just another couple of hours shooting the bull with Mr. Jones. What a waste of time, especially since he knows how many units he's going to take, and I know he knows, and he knows I know he knows."

This is entirely the wrong way to look at things. *Every minute you spend with a prospect or a client is another opportunity to educate that person about what you're selling.* This is especially important when you're in the tech industry, where everything is changing day by day (sometimes minute by minute), but it applies to any sort of sale. Remember: there are constantly new opportunities to show the client the uses of your product or service.

If Mr. Jones doesn't think your product can do what you say it can do, then you've fallen down on this part of the job. To persuade him otherwise, the conversation might start along these lines:

Client: I'm sorry, but we don't need those widgets anymore.

Salesperson: Would you tell me why?

Client: Well, with our new widget-winder, we need a better type of widget, one that can run both forward and backward, and I'm afraid your product doesn't do that.

Salesperson: I see. Well, it's true that this model of widget doesn't do that, but we now carry another model that does. I'd like to demonstrate it, but it would be helpful if you would tell me more about the new widget-winder so I can see just how I can help you.

WHAT IS THE CLIENT *REALLY* SAYING?

Notice that in none of these conversations does the salesperson directly challenge the client ("Well, you're just wrong about that!"). Instead, our experienced and knowledgeable salesperson gently leads the client back to a discussion of what's most important—how can we work together to our mutual benefit?

The lesson in all this is that many times when someone raises an objection to a sale, she's not saying what it sounds like she's saying. You have to listen carefully and then start asking questions, getting her to talk. The more she talks, the better an idea you'll have of the real basis for the objection.

Of course, it's possible that in some circumstances you may not get a sale. If your company just doesn't make what the company wants or needs anymore, you can walk away with a clear conscience—although as I've made clear elsewhere, it doesn't do to slam any doors shut.

SUCCEEDING TOO WELL

Not long ago I ran into this particular objection on a call I made to a client. The company used my services in training their sales force for several years, and I called to set up the annual training session, confident that it was going to take no longer than five or ten minutes.

Instead, the vice president of sales hemmed and hawed and finally got around to it. "I'm sorry, Steve," he said, "but I just don't think we'll need you this year."

I gripped the phone tighter and took a sip of coffee to calm myself. "That's too bad," I said. "Would you tell me why?"

"Well," he said, "frankly you did such a great job the past couple of years that our numbers have gone way up. But I talked to the department manager, and his feeling was that since there hasn't been any turnover in the sale staff since the last time you were here, there's not anything more you can teach these guys." His voice quickened, "So I really appreciate the call, but now . . ."

I broke one of my cardinal rules of phone calls and interrupted him. "That's great that the numbers are so much improved. I'm glad to hear that. But would you tell me a bit more about what techniques the sales force is using that are particularly working for them? That would really be helpful to me in planning future training sessions. I always like to get feedback on what worked."

He started *um*-ing and *er*-ing again, while I waited patiently. In the end, he connected me with the sales manager, and I was able to make my pitch that, given the success of my training methods, it would benefit the salespeople if I reinforced what was working and we had a discussion about what wasn't. I wound up scheduling the training session, and it was a big success—for me *and* the company.

WHO MAKES THIS OBJECTION?

Let's end by taking a look at how our four groups will voice the objection about not needing the product or service and how this will condition your reaction.

1. *Dominant.* This group is often inclined to throw out this objection as a way of testing you, deciding how much you really know about your product and how determined you are to make a sale. "I don't need this!" they'll say, and wait for your reaction. You'd better have all your research at the tips of your fingers, because this group is going to want hard facts and figures to back up your arguments. But they'll also respect you for pushing back because they react positively to strength.

2. *Influence.* Members of this group want to like you, so they're hasty to assure you that their lack of interest in what you're selling has nothing personal about it. Their people-pleasing skills may be so overwhelming that you'll be half-way out of the building before you realize that you've been left with no sale. At the same time, this group, more than the other three, is open to the viewpoint that "we're all in this together for the win." You'll need to persuade them that your product or service is, in fact, just what they need.

3. *Steadiness.* The inherently conservative nature of this group—born of the fact that they hate, hate, *hate* to make a decision—means that they tend to use a lot of objections as obstacles to a sale, whether accurate or not. If you're speaking to a group that falls in this category, be sure to come back over and over again to the issue: What do they

really need? If they don't need this product, perhaps there's something else you can sell them. If they don't need anything in this whole category, what types of products or services *would* be of assistance to them?

4. *Conscientious.* The chief difficulty with this group is getting a reaction. They can feel like an energy drain, the last thing you want during a presentation. However, they also rely heavily on facts and figures (like the Dominant group, whom they strongly resemble in this regard), so they'll be most impressed if you can show, through statistics, that this objection is invalid. When talking to a group of Conscientious clients, your extensive research into the company and industry will always pay off.

WE DON'T NEED SOME OF THE PRODUCT'S FEATURES

W hen I was younger, newspapers and magazines regularly ran stories on the subject of the future. In the future, they assured us, in addition to having cured cancer, world hunger, and war, science would produce an amazing range of products that would make all of our lives easier.

Heading the list was flying cars. In the twenty-first century—maybe even by the closing decade of the twentieth—every American family would own a hover car. Roads would become obsolete, and we'd zoom over woods and water in luxurious, air-conditioned comfort. This idea was so prevalent that in the 1980s it was even worked into the storyline of the movie *Back to the Future* in which Michael J. Fox and Christopher Lloyd, transported to 2015, travel in a flying car.

The year 2015 isn't that far away, and I, for one, want to know where my flying car is. However, in thinking about it, perhaps it's not such a bad thing that we don't all have cars that can whiz through the air at 80 miles an hour. Accidents on the road today are bad enough without adding a third dimension to our daily traveling. So if I were to buy a car and the salesperson were to offer me a "hover button," I'd probably tell him that's not a feature I need or am interested in.

I bring this up because these days, with technology changing so rapidly that it's almost impossible to keep up, it's easy for companies to start manufacturing products that include dozens of new features. Every time, for instance, that I consider buying a new cell phone I have to wade through an explanation of all the new things this or that model can do that were unheard of just a few short months before. If you believe the advertising, it won't be long before we can use our phones not only to call other people but also do anything else with them, from shopping, to texting, to riding them on the surf in Maui. What the phone companies never seem to stop and ask themselves is, how many customers really *want* this kind of stuff? I mean, I like my Black-Berry as much as the next person, but after I'm done making phone calls, checking my e-mail, and sending a few messages in reply to particularly urgent queries or requests, I'm ready to put the thing in my pocket. So why do I need all these other features?

Computer software seems peculiarly prone to this sort of thing. A company will make a program for, say, word processing and then add a feature that allows the user to translate his prose into Esperanto at the click of a button. Maybe someone in the software developer's firm thought this was a neat idea, but from the consumer's point of view, it's a useless frill.

WHAT DOES THE CUSTOMER REALLY WANT?

Before you call on the customer, before you pick up the phone to make the appointment, you've got to research, to decide *exactly* what problems the customer has that you're trying to help her or him solve. That's the key to making a sale. You sell from an intimate knowledge of the client's customer base, sales patterns, manufacturing structure, and position within the industry. *You must know these issues at least as well as the client if you want to make consistent sales.*

If you do this properly, you'll have already anticipated this objection and have the answer at your fingertips. When the client tells you that she doesn't need some of the features, you can explain with specific examples how these are going to improve her company's performance and bring quantitative benefits to her. The conversation should go something like this:

> *Client:* I appreciate your making a pitch today, and I can certainly see that your widget has a lot of fine features. But the problem is that we really don't need most of these features, and we can get a widget without them for a much cheaper per-unit price.
>
> *Salesperson:* I see. Would you tell me which of these features you're concerned about?

(*Note*: You start with a request for information. Don't assume anything; instead, let the client set the framework for the discussion.)

> *Client:* Well, for instance, your widget comes in four different colors, but this isn't something our customers are concerned about. They're happy to just buy widgets in the color we sell.
>
> *Salesperson:* Really? That's interesting. I have some research here [digging in his briefcase] that suggests that in firms that offer a selection of colors, widget sales have increased

by 15 percent over the year. In light of that number, why do you think your customers don't care about color selection?

(*Note:* Don't contradict the customer or become confrontational. That's not going to get you anywhere except on your way out the front door. Rather, present facts and figures that show the value of the feature.)

Client: Well, that might be the case. But take this other aspect of the widget. Our customers aren't interested in that sort of thing, and it just adds to the price.

Salesperson: Hmm. Well, suppose I could show you that in fact widgets without this feature are priced at or above our widget? Would that make a difference in your opinion?

Client: It might. But you'd have to prove to me that it would improve sales. You'd have to show me that customers really want this kind of functionality.

Salesperson: I think the best way to discuss this is to focus on what customers do with the widget. Let's go through that, and I believe I can show you that this function will enhance the customer experience and make them happier with its performance. And as you know, happy customers are repeat customers.

(*Note:* Again, the focus is on facts. It's also notable that the salesperson has turned the discussion to what the client's customers are getting out of their use of the product and how this will benefit the client by bringing in repeat customers.)

HOW DOES THE CLIENT INTEND
TO USE THE PRODUCT?

One of the first tasks is to determine precisely what the client is trying to do with the product. This might seem obvious, but there are times when even the client is in a fog about it.

A friend of mine used to work for a large company that made a variety of products. One day, the head of project management called a meeting to announce, with a grand flourish, that his team had purchased a new software program that was going to make the scheduling of all products within the company much easier. He declared that they would implement it first on the biggest and most important product the company made and then move down to smaller, less-important products, implementing the new scheduling system throughout the company.

My friend, who had a good instinct for B.S., waited patiently for several months. Finally, he was called into a meeting with the head of project management, who said it was time to implement the scheduling software. My friend, who had been doing some investigating on his own, pointed out that the new software not only wouldn't work with his production schedule and needs but if it were implemented it would actually *increase* the lead time necessary for the product, doing the exact opposite of what was intended.

There was a painful silence, which my friend broke by asking, "How's this system working out in X department [the big, important product's area]?"

The project manager looked very embarrassed and said, "Well, to tell you the truth we haven't been able to implement it there, because it turns out that the product has too many scheduling phases for the software to handle."

My friend didn't have to hear anything more. It was obvious what had happened. The project management department had purchased a product without a clear-cut use for it, without knowing enough about its properties and limitations. Now they were stuck with it, scrambling to find somewhere—*anywhere*—in the company where they could implement it and justify its cost.

When my friend told me this story over drinks several months after the fact—and after the head of project management had been let go from the company—my instinct was to blame the manager for making a foolish purchase without thinking it through. But in discussing it and considering it more, I came to the conclusion that the salesperson who sold it to the manager was equally to blame. She or he should have asked the basic question: *What do you intend to do with this product?* Only after getting a clear answer to that should they have proceeded with the sale. True, the salesperson sold an expensive piece of software and probably made a healthy commission. But the company, having been once burned, was now twice shy, and the salesperson lost a long-term customer.

The point is that sometimes the client doesn't know which features of the product are going to be of use and which aren't because he hasn't thought through exactly what he's going to do with it. This is an important opportunity for you to discuss with him and together decide what's useful and what isn't and what kind of product will be best for the client's needs.

HOW WELL DOES THE CLIENT KNOW THE INDUSTRY?

Sometimes—and this happens particularly when you're selling to small businesspeople—the problem isn't so much that they don't know their customers but that they don't know the industry. Imagine, for instance, someone who enters the graphic design business. She's got a staff of designers cranking out work for clients. But she herself isn't in the business because she's a great designer. She's the one with the money to invest and the business sense to get it all together. The problem is, if she doesn't consult her designers, she may have a very limited idea of what features they need for their design software. She also may have only an incomplete knowledge of what kind of design programs are in use throughout the graphic design industry.

Again, you need to ask questions. You need to determine just how well the client knows what uses the product will be put to and what the prevailing industry standards are.

Finally, it may be that after all these discussions and questions, you'll come to the conclusion that the client's right: her customers *don't* need all those features. But does that mean that the sale is over?

Not necessarily. First, and most obviously there's the question of whether you can strip the product of the features that are unwanted. Second, there's the possibility that the product can be used by another part of the company or for another purpose. Consider both of these points before you give up and walk away.

WHO MAKES THIS OBJECTION?

Any one of our four groups can make the objection about not needing a product's features, but your approach to them will be different.

1. *Dominant.* The overwhelming instinct of this group is skepticism, so they may raise this objection as part of their

general critique of the product. In that case, this isn't likely to be the main objection, just one of a number. Because of their reliance on hard data, you can convince this group if you can show that each feature of the product has a specific benefit to their customers, one that will result in increased revenues for them.

2. *Influence.* In some respects, this will be the group that's easiest to convince because they are probably the most in touch with their customers. Their networking instincts lead them to maintain a strong relationship with the customer base, and they are most open to your explanation of customer benefits. On the other hand, precisely because they know the customer base so well, you need to pay careful attention when they raise this objection and decide if it's got any validity behind it.

3. *Steadiness.* Wishy-washy people are hard to persuade of anything, but this group is particularly difficult. In some respects, they are both the most likely to raise this objection—because it helps them avoid making a decision—and at the same time the ones for whom this objection is the least valid. You'll have to spend a lot more time with them, but in the end once you convince them, they are likely to stay convinced. In this respect they are different from, for example, Dominants, whose questioning will continue unabated through every stage of your sale and long afterward.

4. *Conscientious.* Nope. They just can't see it. Why would the customers want A, B, or C features? It's not going to happen. This group tends to project onto their customers the same lack of enthusiasm that drives them. It's particularly

important with this group to get them to talk about what the customers do with the product and what drives them. In this way, they'll gradually expand their own understanding of the needs of their customer base. But you can't tell them about it; you've got to lead them to that understanding themselves.

THIS ISN'T THE KIND OF THING OUR CUSTOMERS NEED

Some time ago, my computer gave out. I'd seen it coming for a while. The keys were sticking, the screen was getting duller, and simple operations took forever. Matters finally came to a head when the machine managed to lose an important document I'd spent the better part of a week working on. I knew at that point that our long relationship had finally come to an end.

The next day, I made my way to the local computer store to get a new machine. Now, I'm not a high-tech kind of guy, so I wasn't looking for anything with a lot of bells and whistles, just a reliable, fast, easy-to-work computer.

The minute I stepped through the door, two salespeople converged on me. I don't know if they were having a slow day or what, but both of them started speaking at once, almost literally pulling me in two different directions.

I got out from between them and turned to the younger one, a pleasant-looking young fellow in his twenties.

"I want—," I started to say.

He interrupted me. "Let me show you what we've got here." He led the way, almost bouncing with excitement. "This is our newest machine," he announced proudly. "We've only got three of these in stock. This is great for gaming and for doing Web design. It's got a graphics card that puts other computers to shame. And you'll be amazed how clear the graphics are for MMOs"

I felt as if I were getting lost in a fog. "MMOs?" I groped.

"Massive Multiplayer Online Games." He gave me a look as if I was feebleminded. "You know. *World of Warcraft?*"

I shook my head. "No, that's not what I want. I don't play games, and I don't need graphics. I need a computer to write with and to send e-mails."

He looked at me as if I'd stepped out of the Stone Age. "Don't you *want* to play games on it?" he asked. "And these days everyone's doing a lot of animation and embedded hyperlinks, even if they're just . . . *writing*. To do that, you'll need a machine like this. This is the *best*. Don't you want the *best*?"

I shook my head again. "No. What I want is really simple. A good, basic machine for writing and e-mailing. I write books on sales and selling and . . ."

His attention had already wandered away. He turned and walked off in search of another customer.

And I walked out the door.

WHAT DO YOU *REALLY* WANT?

This incident brought home to me one of the basic problems with a lot of salespeople. *They aren't concerned with what the client really wants.* And that's the main reason why the objection that's the subject of this chapter comes up.

The positive corollary to my story about the computer is that the next store I went in, the salesperson started off by asking what I was going to use the computer for and then, based on that, proceeded to ask me a bunch of other questions about my storage capacity requirements, speed, any other programs I was interested in, and finally, after all that, showed me several computers that fit my requirements.

The basic lesson is this: don't focus on the product; focus on the client.

If you've made your pitch and the first thing the client says is, "This isn't the kind of thing our customers want," it's a sure sign that you've failed to do the proper research. So let's talk about that.

Before making a sales call, you will research the company you're selling to. These are among the questions to ask:

- "Who are your customers?"

- "Is the business expanding or contracting?"

- "What's your position in the industry?"

- "What's the corporate structure?"

- "What is your current financial status?"

There are lots more questions, of course, but these will do to start.

Each of these questions will break down into a series of subquestions. For example, when you research who the client's customers are, you'll ask:

- "What are these customers' primary needs?"

- "What are their secondary needs?"

- "What are their demographics?"

- "How loyal are they to you?"

The Internet has made this kind of research much easier than it was formerly. You can and should visit your client's Web site, as well as look at magazine and newspaper articles online that contain information about it. Look at its annual reports and other financial information that's public. If the company is publicly traded, research its stock price over the past few years. Note down all your information about the company in a file and review it carefully before you set out on your sales call.

ASK QUESTIONS DURING THE SALES CALL

Even though you've done your research, that's no reason to avoid asking questions when you're talking to the client. In fact, questioning is the most important thing you can do during any sales call.

It's a basic rule of trial lawyers that you should never ask a witness a question to which you don't already know the answer. So during a sales call there's nothing wrong with asking questions that you've already researched. First, it gets you into a conversation with the client, and conversations lead to sales openings and buy signals. Second, it's possible that your research was incorrect or at least didn't uncover all the facts. This sort of conversation can give you a lot of valuable insights into the company's inner workings.

Keep in mind the 80/20 rule. In an ideal sales conversation, you should do 20 percent of the talking and the client should do 80 percent. Thinking back to my experience in the first computer store I went to for my recent purchase, I don't think my part of the conversation even got near 20 percent. The salesperson completely dominated the discussion. As a result, he didn't find out anything about what I wanted. Consequently, he didn't make the sale.

So, one of the first questions to ask during a sales call is, "What do your customers need from the product or service that I'm trying to sell you?"

You can phrase this more generally:

- "Tell me about your customers."

- "Would you explain to me what your customers want?"

- "How would you say your customers use the products we supply?"

In general, always ask open-ended questions rather than closed ones, to which there's only a yes or no answer.

WHEN THE CLIENT SAYS NO

The point I've been making in this chapter is that your goal should be to discourage the client from raising this objection at all. But sometimes, despite your research, it comes up. And you're faced with the problem of keeping the discussion going.

The *wrong* approach is to attempt to change the customer's needs to fit the product. That's what the first computer salesperson tried to do to me. He wanted to tell me that despite my explanation of why I needed his product, I didn't know what I was talking about. As though I didn't *really* understand my own needs. Taking that approach only caused me to put my guard up, since it implied that he was a lot smarter than I was. But even if he'd been successful and bullied me into a sale, the product wouldn't have been the right fit for me. Dissatisfaction would have niggled away at me, and the next time I needed a computer, I would have gone elsewhere.

So if the client says, "This isn't what our customers want," don't argue. Instead, ask the obvious question: "What *do* your customers want?"

The answer may surprise you. Moreover, it tells you a lot about the client's relationship with her or his customers. Further discussion may not only help you better understand the client's customers, it may also give the client some new information about her customers and what they need and want.

Adapting Your Offer

The next step is to figure out if there's a way that your product or service can be adapted to meet these needs. This can be very tricky, depending on the nature of the product. But there should be at least a bit of wiggle room to adjust things. After all, if your product has nothing to do with what the client's customers want, then why are you sitting in the room at all?

The third step is to determine if there's another product or service your company provides that would better address the client's customers' wants. Again, this can be challenging, but it's very necessary. Remember that your goal is to get the client something that *best meets his or her needs*. This should be a win-win deal for both of you. The client should feel that she or he has made a purchase that will solve a problem. And for you, of course, there's the advantage of making a significant sale, with the promise of more to come. Those sorts of sales are the basis of an enduring relationship.

It's possible, of course, that there won't be any way to meet this objection. Perhaps the client's business has moved on and your research is out of date (although if that's the case, you should look carefully at your research methods and sources). Even in this case, you want to be careful not to slam any doors. Thank the client politely and suggest that you stay in touch. Then go back to your desk and think about what products you've got under development that might meet the client's future needs. Send him or her a follow-up e-mail, updating progress on the product's development. In the long run, you'll find that this sort of cultivation pays off.

WHO MAKES THIS OBJECTION?

What about our four groups? As always, anyone can make the objection, but some types are more likely to blurt it out than others. Here's how our four groups deal with the objection that the product isn't the kind of thing their customers need.

1. *Dominant.* This type won't have any hesitation in telling you if she thinks you've gone off the rails as far as her customers are concerned. She's going to constantly question you about the product's specific benefits and results. Because these types of clients work best when they're reacting to you—jabbing and poking at your presentation to see if it's sound—you may have some trouble getting them to talk freely about what their customers want. But persistence pays off. Open-ended questions are especially important in persuading them to start talking.

2. *Influence.* A client of this type is closely in touch not only with you but also with her customer base. She wants to bring all of you together in a happy circle. So her concern that your product isn't what her customers want must be taken very seriously. She'll find persuasive your attempts to figure out how your product or service can benefit her customers because it coincides with what she herself wants.

3. *Steadiness.* This is a group in whose hands this objection may actually not be entirely legitimate. The reason is that they're so cautious that they may well be overinterpreting their customers' likes and dislikes. Careful, probing questioning is the key to getting at them, leading them through a detailed discussion of customer psychology. You won't get anywhere pressing them for a fast decision—it's just not in their nature to make one. But the more they talk, with your guidance, the more apt they are to see that your product can be adapted to the customers' needs. They'll also probably be open to a continuing future relationship even if the sale doesn't go through, since it doesn't require an immediate decision from them.

4. *Conscientious.* This group is convinced from the outset that whatever you're selling is not what's needed. They approach everything from the standpoint of what's wrong with it, not what's good about it. For that reason, they, like Steadiness clients, are particularly prone to this objection. But if you can show through specific demonstration and information that the product will benefit their customers, you can bring them around to accept a sale.

IT'S NOT GOOD ENOUGH

How many times has this happened to you?

You make a sales presentation. Your slides are compelling, you've thought through all the benefits your product will bring to the client, you've done your research and know that what you're proposing for an initial order is well within the company's budget. You run through the sales pitch, come to a flourishing conclusion, and sit down, confident that you've just made a big part of your commission for the year.

Then the client looks at you, deadpan, and says, "I'm sorry, but this product just doesn't measure up to our standards."

It's as if you're in an elevator that's gone into freefall. Racing through your head are all the things you could say to rescue the situation, but nothing comes out.

And the client stands up, signaling the conclusion of the meeting and the end of your hopes.

What went wrong?

Now, sometimes, sadly, your company's product *is* not up to the standards that are demanded by the client. If that's true, and true *consistently*, my advice to you is simple: start looking for another employer. Because any company that manufactures a product or provides a service that's below that demanded by industry standards isn't going to stay in business very long.

But I'm assuming you're like most salespeople: you believe in your company and you believe in what you're selling. In fact, you should do that, because that's a basic part of being a good salesperson. You have to believe that what you're providing will solve the client's problem.

Nonetheless, in the aftermath of a meeting such as the one I've just described, you need to sit down and do a serious comparison of your product or service versus the needs of your client. Be as objective as possible and try to measure the gap between the two. If there is a split, and it's substantial, then the time has come for a talk with your boss about the problem.

IT'S NOT ABOUT QUALITY

Let's assume that you conclude that your product or service does what it says it will do and does it within the generally accepted standards of the industry. Where to go from here?

Well, you could walk away from the client, write him off as a lost cause, and go on to someone who *will* appreciate what you're selling. But in doing so, you're walking away from a potential sale. It's my contention that, in all likelihood, your client doesn't really object to the quality of what you're selling. Rather, what he doesn't like is its function.

Let me give an example:

A salesperson for a paper company makes a presentation to a company that sells greeting cards. The executive for the greeting card company, after listening to the presentation, says, "Well, that's very interesting that you sell card stock like that, but it's not good enough for what we do."

The salesperson, who has read this book and listened to my advice, isn't put off by the answer. Instead, she says, "Would you explain to me, please, a little more about what you do that makes this product inadequate? I want to be sure that we're not talking at cross purposes here, because I've researched your company, and I think this stock would work for the kind of cards you produce."

The company executive hems and haws for a few minutes and then explains: the company has decided recently to move from the basic greeting card format to one that involves recorded messages that play when the recipient opens the card. So when Grandma opens the card from her grandson, a cute little voice will say, "Hi, Grandma! Happy birthday!" And there will be a little tune in the background. These cards are becoming extremely popular, and the company sees a big future in producing them—not only basic recorded greetings but eventually greetings that can be customized to the point that the grandchild can actually record his own greeting to Grandma.

It is a powerful concept, and one that can mean a substantially new market for the company's product. But it means that the greeting card company will need to move to a much heavier stock than the paper it had used previously. After all, the record-and-play device now has to be hidden within the card, and the card has to be sturdy enough to protect it from the vagaries of the postal system.

So, when the salesperson presented a proposal that the greeting card company buy a much lighter stock, the executive's natural response was, "I'm sorry, it's not good enough."

Having gotten this explanation from the executive, the sales rep thinks on her feet. She knows her paper company doesn't sell a stock that is sufficiently heavy to meet the greeting card company's needs. But she also knows that with a little effort it can make a deal with one of its suppliers to meet the demand. The conversation that follows goes something like this:

> *Salesperson:* I think I can get you want you need for this type of card. When would you need delivery?
>
> *Executive:* We're on a crash schedule with these cards, so we'd need to take delivery of 3,000 units in two months.
>
> *Salesperson:* That's pretty tight, but I believe we can do it. Just so I'm clear, you'd want delivery in two months of 3,000 units, and you'd be willing to pay a premium for meeting that aggressive schedule?
>
> *Executive:* How big a premium?
>
> *Salesperson:* We'd be looking at $0.60 per sheet.
>
> *Executive:* That's high. Can we go to $0.30 per sheet?
>
> *Salesperson:* How about if we meet in the middle and say $0.45 per sheet?
>
> *Executive:* You've got a sale.

Notice that the key to this sale is the salesperson's ability to figure out what the greeting card company executive actually wants. She doesn't start from any assumptions; she simply asks. And she's aggressive enough to ask for a higher price since this is a rush schedule and a product that her company doesn't normally carry (although if the account in this case is big enough, the company probably will start to stock it).

The really important point is that by asking a question she gets the sale off "stop" or "close" and begins a dialogue—one that eventually will result in a sale.

Throughout all the books I've written in my decades in this business, there's one point I keep coming back to over and over again, and this objection is a perfect example of it: *you've got to ask the clients questions.* That's the only realistic way you're going to understand what they're really objecting to.

PURSUE THE POINT

Naturally, not everything is this clear-cut. Sometimes, when a prospective sale tells you that your product isn't good enough for her, you've got to probe and push a bit. It's a bit like dentistry. You're sitting in the chair, and the doctor is bent over you, poking at your teeth with instruments that look as if they were developed by one of the nastier branches of the Spanish Inquisition, saying, "Does that hurt?"

Think of this process as a bit like that one. Except that you, as the sales rep, are the dentist. And, if possible, you don't want to make the client scream.

What you do have to do is figure out what aspect of the client's need your product isn't meeting—and, of course, if there's anything you can do about it.

For example, consider the following discussion:

Client: Thanks for the presentation. It's very persuasive, but this service doesn't meet our needs. I appreciate you coming in to talk to me. Now . . .

Salesperson: I understand. And I certainly appreciate you taking the time to listen to me. But before we wrap this up, I wonder if you would tell me in what way our service doesn't measure up to what you need.

Client: Well, it's just not really what we're looking for.

Salesperson: I see. Is it the cost that's a concern?

Client: No, not really. It's more the . . .

Salesperson: Yes?

Client: More the scope of the service, really.

Salesperson: You mean you're looking for something expanded.

Client: Right . . .

Salesperson (who's done her research): Of course. I understand that your current vendor is providing next-day delivery. Is that right?

Client: Yes. And what we need is something better.

Salesperson: Do you mean same-day delivery?

Client: Yes, that's it.

Salesperson: Well, I can certainly look into that for you. Let me ask you, would you be willing to pay a bit more for a guarantee of same-day service? More than you're currently paying your vendor?

Client: I suppose so, if it were absolutely guaranteed.

Salesperson: Okay. I can take that up with my boss. How about if we talk again tomorrow when I've had a chance to speak with him, and we'll see what we can work out?

Client: Okay, that'd be fine.

There are a couple of points to notice about this. First, the problem doesn't become apparent right away. The salesperson has to work to uncover it. It takes a bit of questioning (and sometimes it takes a *lot* of questioning) to get at the real objection.

Second, the salesperson isn't promising anything. There's no "oh, we can fix that for you!" After all, it's a serious business to commit your company to something that's not within your normal parameters of business. Rather, the salesperson establishes some possibilities. The client would be willing to pay a bit more *if* the vendor were willing to extend the range of service. That does two things: first, it gives the salesperson something to take back to her boss; second, and most important, it provides a continuing basis for the dialogue with the client.

That should be one of your overwhelming concerns in any sales call: *don't let it end without a basis for reopening discussion.* In this case, the salesperson makes a specific proposal for when the client and rep can talk again and tosses in the general subject matter of the discussion: whether, for an increase in price, the vendor can increase the scope of service. All in all, this turns what could have been a dead-end failure into something that still holds out the promise of success.

There's nothing more discouraging than to find out that the person whom you thought you were wowing with your eloquence and command of the facts is, in fact, not interested from the beginning. But (as I hope you realize from this chapter) an objection isn't an objection, as long as you can continue the discussion at a later date.

WHO MAKES THIS OBJECTION?

Finally, let's take a quick look at how our different customers might approach the objection that "it's not good enough" and how we might deal with them. Remember that a great part of your success depends on tailoring not only your presentation but also your discussion and negotiation style to the particular personality of your target buyer.

1. *Dominant.* The dominant buyer is convinced of the truth of his own statements and not inclined to let you talk him out of an existing conviction. If your product is not good enough, that's all there is to it. However, this buyer is also apt to react to specific facts, if they can be backed up. So, in this case, you want to explain that although you can't give an answer right now about changing the service or product, you might be able to do so at a later time. If possible, have some examples of times in the past you altered the terms of service or the uses or designs of the product to accommodate a client. Have facts and figures to show how these benefited the client's bottom line.

2. *Influence.* It's probably going to be somewhat easier to get these people to talk to you about the problem; they love to talk. The difficulty is that in their anxiousness to please you and connect with you, they may not tell you what the real problem is. Instead, they've got a tendency to say what they think you want to hear. That can result in short-term gains for you (i.e., a sale), but if you let it go, it's going to create huge problems later on when your product or service doesn't do what they need it to.

3. *Steadiness.* The difficulty is getting this group to explain what the problem is. They're willing to talk, but they're anxious for your understanding and approval, so they're less likely than Group 1, for example, to tell you flat out that your service or product is falling short. This is yet another

case where you'll have to probe and probe until you're confident you've gotten to the heart of the problem.

4. *Conscientious.* These people will drive you crazy if you let them, because it's so hard to get them to agree to continue the dialogue. They want to cut off the discussion because they genuinely don't see it leading anywhere. The best approach is to be positive and full of alternatives. For example: "If A doesn't work, how about if we were to try B? That's no good? Well, what about C?" The most important thing with this group is to ensure that a follow-up meeting takes place in which you can present them with improvements to the product, and prove to them that it now does what they need it to.

YOUR PRODUCT OR
SERVICE IS OUTDATED

7

'll let you in on a secret: I'm not as young as I used to be.

For a long time I just assumed that it wasn't a matter of me getting older. Everyone else was just getting younger. Somehow everything had changed. Stairs got steeper and longer. People talked more quietly and mumbled a lot. But then I finally realized it wasn't them. It was me.

After a certain amount of denial, I did, in fact, come to terms with getting older, and now I'm mostly fine with it. I've had a great life. I've got a grandchild and a loving family. I've had a chance for a wonderful career and met thousands of fascinating people, many of whom have become good friends. No, all in all, it's not been bad.

But there's no doubt things have changed, and as you make your way through the sales landscape, you're bound to encounter some clients who feel that way, too.

THE GOOD OLD DAYS

Not to get overly nostalgic, but there are times when I long for the Good Old Days.

When computers were giant machines that occupied whole buildings at the Massachusetts Institute of Technology.

When telephones sat firmly on our desks and were made of bakelite, heavy enough to bash someone over the head with in a detective story.

When television consisted of three networks and "UHF," a series of channels that depended on manipulating a circular antenna on the back of the set.

When the Internet wasn't even a glint in someone's eye.

Whenever I get into this mood, though, I think about the changes that have come about in my profession. The fact is that sales strategies today are more efficient and in most respects better than they used to be. The Internet and the speed of communication mean that it's easier for salespeople to assemble information with which to make an intelligent and informed pitch. It means we can react faster to market trends and that we can find out with the speed of light the answer to issues regarding delivery or supply.

Most young salespeople today would be amazed by the kinds of challenges that faced salespeople when I started out in this profession more than three decades ago. "How on Earth," I hear them ask, "did you guys ever sell *anything*?"

TIMES CHANGE

All of this is good to keep in mind when someone tells you your product or service is outdated. Knowing this serves to remind us that the pace of change has increased to a blinding speed.

This pace has been captured in several "laws."

Moore's Law, named after Intel founder Gordon Moore, says that the number of computer transistors than can be placed on an integrated circuit doubles every two years; this means that the speed and power of computers is increasing exponentially.

The *Law of Accelerating Returns*, proposed by futurist Ray Kurzweil, says that *all* technological change increases exponentially. If that is the case, then we can expect the future in 50 years to be vastly different not only from anything we know now but from anything we can imagine.

So when you've made a pitch for your product and the client tells you that what you're selling is outdated, you have to keep in mind that being outdated is part of the general scheme of things these days.

Of course, that doesn't make the objection any easier to hear. After all, you believe in what you're selling. (If you don't, you shouldn't be selling it. I make this point in other chapters and other books; a good salesperson *must* believe in the value of whatever she or he is selling. Otherwise, rethink your career.) So it's never good to hear that it's outdated.

FIND OUT WHAT THEY KNOW

Step one when confronted with this objection is to determine the facts. And the number one question to ask is this: does the client really know what she or he is talking about? So, start asking questions.

There's no call to do so in a confrontational or aggressive way. If you ask along the lines of, "Do you really know that this product is out of date, or are you just blowing smoke?" the conversation is going to end right then and there. Instead, try to find out what the client means by asking two things: What does the product or service *not* do that you need it to do? Would you give me an example of a product or service that *does* do what you need it to do?

The answers to these two questions are going to give you a lot of information about how much the client really knows. It's entirely possible, in the event that you're dealing with people from the upper levels of the corporate hierarchy, that they're simply relaying what they've been told by the folks down in research and developement. If that's the case, they'll probably flounder around a bit and get mired in generalities. On the other hand, in small companies where the executive officers are more intimately involved with their customer base, they probably know the ins and outs of it, and they can tell you exactly what your product can and can't do for them.

The next step is to find out the client's familiarity with the state of the industry. After all, if they're telling you that what you're presenting is out of date, they must have an idea of how your competition is dealing with these problems.

Although the CEO of a big company may not be readily familiar with all the details of precisely what his customers are looking for, he should know a lot about his industry. Sadly, some don't, and your questions should separate the wheat from the chaff.

Ignorance versus Knowledge

If the CEO (or another corporate bigwig you're pitching to) isn't sure exactly why your product is out of date, because either he doesn't know his customer base or he doesn't know his industry (or both), you can move to retake control of the sale. Don't be explicit about his ignorance, but make it clear that you're not going to let him get away with it. Your pitch can go like this:

"I can sympathize with your concerns that you need to have the most up-to-date service possible so that you're competitive and your customers feel they're getting the best value for their money. However, I can assure you that our service more than meets these standards. For instance [here, explain in detail the benefits your service provides and the problems it solves]. No one else in the industry comes close to dealing with these issues on this level."

A clear-headed, knowledgeable representation of your product or service and its benefits will turn back an ill-founded objection of this type and give you the upper hand in the sale.

On the other hand, if the client *is* speaking to you from a position of knowledge, your problem becomes more complicated: it suggests a weakness in your presentation.

In short: *you should know your product better than anyone—* better than the client, better than your competition. Knowledge is power, and your advantage in any sale is the amount you know about what you're selling. So, if your product or service has really fallen behind what the industry can offer, you've got further work to do to educate yourself.

It's a difficult situation in which to find yourself, but here's what I recommend:

1. *Collect as many facts as possible.* Since the client is the expert at this point, find out from him or her precisely what the most advanced product in your field can do. Try to narrow the list down to three or four salient points that you can jot down on a single side of a notepad page.

2. *Look for further resources.* Ask the client if it would be possible to talk to anyone within the company who might be able to give you more insights into what kind of product functions they're looking for. Especially if you're dealing with a top executive, she or he may be very willing to kick you downstairs to a more junior member of the team who's closer to actual customers and knows what they want.

3. *Set another appointment.* As always when you meet an object-ion, the key objective is not to end the sale. Say something along the lines of, "Well, you've given me a lot to think about. I'd like to continue this after I consult with our R&D staff about how we can meet your concerns. Would next Thursday at 3 p.m. be a good time for our next appointment?"

4. *Follow up.* As soon as you get back to the office, follow up with a note to the client reiterating your desire to meet his needs and assuring him that you're looking into making your prod-uct the instrument that does so.

TALK TO YOUR PEOPLE

Now you come to the moment of truth. You're going to have to find out from your people if the client's concerns have a basis in reality. In all probability you'll know the answer, since you should know the product and industry better than anyone. But in case you don't, talk to your own people. Tell them what the client said and ask for their reactions. Do research on the state of the industry—has it changed while you were asleep?

Finally, sit down and do some hard thinking about the most basic problem of all: *what does the client need*? After all, this is at the root of the success or failure of your sale.

With this new information and new perspective, it's time to make your second sales call on the client. With proper prepara-tion, it's going to take one of two forms:

1. You'll be able to tell the client that you can adapt your prod-uct or service to his needs, give him a time frame for this, and promote your product as cost effective and functionally

superior to the competition. Doing so is tricky, because any improvement in a product takes time, and time is probably just what the client doesn't have in abundance.

2. You can explain to the client your new perspective on what he needs. It may well be that this need isn't met by the competition's product, even if it's more technically advanced than what you're selling.

As a practical matter, I can tell you that I've run into this objection over the years from people who think my precepts about selling seem very old-fashioned. They're looking for sales training that seems more cutting edge, more focused on the Internet, Twitter, social networking, and so on.

I've listened with interest to what these people say, but then I counter with what I can offer. "Listen," I say, "I know you want a lot more fancy bells and whistles on your sales training. What I'm doing sounds old-fashioned. It's true. I admit it.

"But if it sounds that way, it's because *what's worked in the past works now!* The forms of selling may have changed, but its essence hasn't. We still sell to the same kinds of clients; we still have to go through the same exercises of asking questions, following the 80/20 rule, and finding ways around clients' objections. That's not changed in hundreds of years. So yes, what I do sounds old-fashioned. Because it's rooted in the successes of the past, and that's what you need to sell in the future."

WHO MAKES THIS OBJECTION?

Three of the four groups we've been considering are likely to make the objection that your product or service is outdated; one not so much.

1. *Dominant.* Drawing their aggression and power from data, Dominants pride themselves on being up-to-the-minute on the state of the industry, as well as the details of their company. When they tell you that what you're selling is out of date, be sure to listen carefully, because they almost certainly know what they're talking about. Don't argue; it's only going to make them mad. Instead, thank them for their input and bring it back to your own people.

2. *Influence.* Because of their extensive connections, members of this group are likely to have a good idea of what's standard throughout the industry. Fortunately, they don't have inhibitions about sharing information, so they can give you some excellent insights. Of course, anything you tell them is going to be public knowledge in a matter of days, if not hours.

3. *Steadiness.* This group is less inclined to be involved in the day-to-day functioning of their company. If they do raise this objection, it's more likely to be in the form of a question: "Are you sure this is what we need? I mean, it's not old-fashioned or anything?" Insofar as they stick to the objection, it's likely that it reflects the views of another group within the company, in which case your challenge becomes to find out which group is really raising the roadblock.

4. *Conscientious.* Since this group dislikes change, their natural inclination is toward the tried and true, and thus they tend not to raise this objection. However, they like data, so they'll ask for a lot of information about the product. But when addressing a group made up of Conscientious people, it's often safe to stress the conservative nature of your proposal and its continuity with the company's past.

I REALLY HATE
THE REP

Sometimes, during a pitch, the client will say something so mind-boggling that it throws off the whole conversation. We will see instances of this throughout the book, but it's especially prevalent with the objection I'll discuss in this chapter.

Let me illustrate the idea for you.

A few years ago, a friend of mine went into a company to make a pitch. It was one that his firm had dealt with for a couple of years, and there was an established relationship between the two companies—my friend understood from his boss and from others that it was a good one. He arrived at the company and was greeted by the client, an executive vice president. The two sat down in a conference room, and the salesman pulled out his materials and laid them on the table. He opened his mouth to begin the pitch when the VP interrupted with, "To tell you the truth, I'm not sure there's much point in this. I don't think we're going to buy from you."

The salesperson's stomach turned over and twisted in a double knot. He recovered enough to ask for the reason behind the client's decision. Meanwhile, he was thinking, "This is ridiculous! I haven't even started the pitch yet. How can this guy know what the terms are and make a decision already?"

The VP pushed back from the table and, smiling slightly, said, "It's just that we have a big problem with your company's people. We're not interested in buying from them."

A lot of salespeople would have started a slow boil at this point. After all, this was an attack on the integrity of my friend's company and his colleagues. What was this guy talking about?

Fortunately, the salesperson, being familiar with Schiffman's First Commandment of Selling, didn't start yelling or shovel his materials back into his briefcase and walk out the door. Instead, he started to do what any good salesperson does when confronted with an objection: ask questions and listen.

"I'm sorry to hear that," he said. "Would you tell me what problems you've had? I'd certainly like to help fix whatever problems you've come up in dealing with us."

The VP hemmed and hawed for a few minutes. Then he said, "Well, I have to say that some of it's personal."

My friend nodded encouragingly. "I see," he said. "Would you explain a bit more?"

"To tell you the truth," the VP answered, "our impression here at the ABC Corporation is that your company just doesn't think of us as a very important client. That's the impression we keep getting from your reps."

Wow! That's serious stuff. If there's one thing every salesperson ought to have written in letters of gold over her or his desk, it's that *the client you're selling to is always the most important client on your list.* If the reps from my friend's company weren't doing that, something was very wrong. But my friend didn't want to leave it there. He probed deeper.

"That's very concerning," he said. "I can assure you that to me you're a *very* important client. But would you tell me what the reps have done to give you that impression?"

Then it started to come out:

1. The reps had overpromised and underdelivered, especially when it came to the service aspects of the product. The company had gradually come to think that if the rep said one thing, the reality was only going to be about 50 percent of that promise—if that.

2. The reps had not kept up regular contact with the company. Weeks had gone by with virtually no communication. And if that wasn't bad enough, when the company had taken the initiative and called my friend's colleagues, many times those phone calls had gone unanswered.

3. The reps in the past had never seemed as if they were listening. When the VP and others in the ABC Corporation had tried to explain their changing needs, the reps had steamrollered them, implying that they, the reps, knew better what the company's real needs were.

All these things had built up over time to the point where, from ABC Corporation's point of view, my friend's company was toxic. The VP had been chosen to deliver the message that the relationship was at an end.

WHAT WENT WRONG?

If a relationship has degenerated to this extent, very often there's little you can do to rebuild it. In these circumstances, sometimes the best thing to do is to get out and take the lessons back to your company, with the hope of reestablishing the relationship with the client at some point in the future.

My friend, however, decided to see if he might be able to salvage something from all this. He said, "Well, this is all disturbing, and it certainly seems as if you've got some legitimate complaints. I can assure you that I'm taking this very seriously and will address these issues with my superiors as soon as I get back in the office. In the meantime, though, would you tell me what it would take to salvage this relationship to the point that you think you could trust us again?"

The VP thought about it and came up with several suggestions, to which my friend added a few others. Their final pact looked something like this:

- My friend agreed to call the VP once a week to discuss how the product was working and what the company's ongoing needs were.

- They agreed (subject to the approval of their superiors) on a discounted package of services for the product.

- These services would be overseen personally by my friend.

- Once a month, my friend would come to the ABC Corporation for a half hour sit-down with the VP, so they could discuss matters face to face.

When they'd finished, they drew up a document specifying these steps. Both agreed that if their companies approved it, they would each sign this document as the contractual bond of their new working relationship.

This story has a happy ending, although there were some very red faces when my friend returned to his office and informed his boss of how the visit had gone. In the end, two salespeople were demoted and another was fired for their roles in the situation. But the relationship with the client was rebuilt, and the ground was laid for further sales.

WHAT CAN YOU DO?

When this objection comes up, clearly the first thing to do is find out why the problem arose. The biggest question is, does the client have a problem with the previous rep? Or with you?

If it's with you, you'll have to overcome the blow to your ego and find out why. Doing so can be embarrassing and upsetting, since it's never fun to listen to someone dissecting your professional style, your appearance, or the way you eat spaghetti. But you can't move the conversation forward without it.

This comes back to something I've said to the many audiences of salespeople I've trained over the past 30 years: at the end of the day, as a salesperson all you've got is your integrity and your belief in what you're selling.

If the problem is with the previous rep, as was the case in the example I cited previously, then your challenge is both easier and more difficult. It's easier because it's always easier to talk about other people's faults than it is about your own. But it's more difficult because you've got less control over what other people do than over your own actions. If you're the problem, you can fix what's wrong without much fuss. If someone else is the problem, you've got to find a way of repairing what they've done. And that can get complicated.

In rebuilding the relationship, here are some rules:

1. *Don't overpromise.* It's better to be conservative in your estimate of what you can do for the client and then overdeliver. Everyone likes to see their expectations exceeded.

2. *Keep your time frames realistic.* If, as a result of bad salesmanship on the part of previous reps, significant problems have developed, figure out how long it's going to take to fix

them and then add some time to the end of that. Always allow for Murphy's Law: anything that can go wrong, will go wrong.

3. *Don't blame other people.* Even if it's clear that the situation is the result of others' incompetence, don't get into the blame game. It will undermine you as a professional and pull the discussion in the wrong direction. Rather than focusing on people, focus on the problems that need to be solved.

4. *Be honest.* If problems have arisen because of actions you took (or didn't take), step up to the plate and take responsibility. Doing so is always respected, and it will go a long way to fix a damaged relationship.

WHO MAKES THIS OBJECTION?

Turning to our four groups, let's see who's most likely to bring up the point about hating the reps. I should make clear that this problem can arise in any vendor-client relationship, but which type of person brings it up to you is going to shape the way in which you present your solution.

1. **Dominant.** Not surprisingly, these are the people who are most likely to tell you the minute that you or one of your colleagues has screwed up. They're uninhibited about saying flat out, "I won't buy from you because I think you're an incompetent jerk!" It may be hard to get the conversation moving forward after an aggressive statement such as that, but your best bet is total honesty: "All right. Let's talk about that. What makes you think I'm incompetent? What am

I doing that's making you not want to buy from me?" These people are skeptical, so if they've had less-than-satisfactory service or products from your company in the past, just assuring them that you're different isn't going to cut it. You'll have to offer a lot of specifics and information and commitments to back them up before a Dominant client is going to be satisfied.

2. *Influence.* As the ultimate networkers, Influence people don't like to cut anyone out of their group, so they may be reluctant to voice this objection out loud. Particularly if the problem is with you, they want to help you and understand you. You can use this to your advantage, because if you make it very clear that you're willing to change your style of interaction, they'll be inclined to give you a lot of useful feedback. If the problem is with previous reps, you can emphasize the ways in which you, personally, are different. Remember that interaction with this group is on a very personal level, one that seems at times to merge with the professional.

3. *Steadiness.* These customers are less likely to raise this objection, but at the same time it can affect them more than the other groups. Anger or irritation with you or with your fellow salespeople will fester in their minds and poison every aspect of their relationship with your company. Once you bring out the objection through extensive questioning, you'll find that it's a long, hard slog to get them to agree to a plan for rebuilding the relationship. Their caution impels them against the idea that you and your company can change. But a list of specific steps you're willing to take will go a long way toward this goal.

4. *Conscientious.* As the people who don't show much excitement or enthusiasm about anything, these customers may well tell you up front that they hate the rep: they hate her style of selling, the services she's offering, her hairstyle, her clothing, and her perfume. Remember, though, that your job is to get the discussion off personalities and onto concrete steps to fix the problem. Here, the Conscientious customer's need for hard data works very much in your favor. If you can show how the relationship with your company gives specific, quantified benefits to the client's business, that is a persuasive argument for Conscientious clients.

YOUR COMPANY HAS A BAD TRACK RECORD

It's three o'clock on a Thursday afternoon. The salesperson is going through the motions. She's not been confident that she has the sale since the start of the presentation. Heck, she's not been confident about it since she walked through the door and the company's CEO greeted her with a cold-fish handshake and a stare that would have drilled holes through a stainless steel vault. But she knows she's got to keep going because that's what the routine is: make the presentation, answer a few meaningless questions, and get out and get on the way to the next sale, which—the Lord willing—will be easier.

She finishes with a flourish and waits for someone to ask something.

And then the CEO stands up and says, "Thanks for coming in, and I appreciate your time, but I have to tell you that your company has a bad track record with us."

Well, that's it. There's really no point in going on. She's already rehearsing in her mind the speech she's going to make to her boss. "I couldn't do a thing because all the previous reps have just ruined it for us. That company *hates* us now. We should cross them off the list of customers and make up the sales revenue somewhere else."

"IT'S SOMEONE ELSE'S FAULT"

Let's face it: it's always easier to blame someone else when the sale doesn't go through. For that matter, it's easier to shift the burden of responsibility when anything goes wrong. When the client tells you that he or she isn't inclined to buy from you because your company has a record of failure, it's especially easy to assume that your predecessors have simply screwed things up beyond repair. After that, it's a short step to retiring the client to the dead file.

In reality, though, this objection isn't insurmountable. In fact, it's in some respects a good sign, because the very fact that you're there, giving the presentation at all, says that they're willing to give you another chance.

Start off with one of the most basic rules in sales: *don't blame someone else*. Repeat this after me. *Do not blame someone else.*

It never works.

For one thing, it starts you both off on a negative footing. If the client tells you that your company has a bad track record, and you start casting about for whom to blame ("It was the previous CEO. He was a complete loser. Boy, was he bad!"), you're simply focusing all of the client's attention on everything that went wrong. Doing so reinforces the idea that your company can't effectively deal with the problem.

Also, that sort of thing is likely to come back to bite you on the behind. Negativity on your part is going to convince your client of two things: first, that you can't be trusted, since someone who'd rat on his boss is probably saying bad things about his customers as well; second, that you're more interested in shifting responsibility than dealing with the problem.

CONFRONT THE ISSUE

Your most powerful weapon, when confronted with this objection, is your willingness to accept responsibility for your company's actions. After all, you're the company's representative. When the client thinks about the name of your company, yours is the face that comes into her or his mind. So in this situation you've got to step up to the plate. If you won't take ownership of the issue, who will?

That doesn't mean you have to say that *you* failed. Quite the contrary. It means that you have to start by admitting the problem and volunteering responsibility for dealing with it.

Before doing that, though, you must determine exactly what the problem is. The dialogue should go something like this:

Client: Your company has a very bad track record with us.

Salesperson: I'm sorry to hear you say that. We really strive to meet our clients' needs, and I'm disappointed that in your case we obviously fell down on the job. Would you tell me what happened?

Client: When we first signed with you, we had great service for two years. But after that, everything fell off. Your reps stopped returning our calls.

Salesperson: That was when, exactly?

Client: About a year and a half ago. We complained about the drag on service and about the problems with response, but nothing did any good. Right now, I've got to tell you, we're ready to give this contract to someone else who's going to be more responsive.

Salesperson: I hear you. And I certainly understand that you want someone who's going to deal with service issues in a timely manner. Would you tell me something about the level of service you were receiving during the first couple of years when you were satisfied with us?

Notice that the salesperson in this scenario has worked the conversation back around to a positive: the point when the company was providing something that the client liked. This is a useful tactic, because it reminds the client of why he signed with your company in the first place. What's important now is to elicit the particulars of *why* the service fell off.

JUST THE FACTS, MA'AM

Remember the old TV show *Dragnet*? All right, so maybe I'm a bit older than you, and I remember it. On the show, Lt. Joe Friday of the Los Angeles Police Department questioned witnesses and suspects alike with the same deadpan stare. And his signature line was always, "Just the facts, Ma'am." (Or Sir, as the case might be.)

In other words, no opinions. Just tell me what's going on and I'll take it from there.

That's your job in this situation. Don't offer opinions and explanations. Don't try to assign blame or proffer excuses. There's no need for that. What you need is the facts—just the facts.

The facts are going to tell you what went wrong and give you some important clues about how to fix it. They're also going to move the discussion off an emotional level and make it a rational exchange of views on how to improve the situation. It badly needs that, because this objection is emotionally loaded. So, when the client starts to give you a recitation of all the things that have gone wrong over the past couple of years and how they've all mounted up to his lack of confidence in your company, do your best to keep him on the facts. Just the facts.

FIXING THE PROBLEM

Once you've got the facts, the next step is to determine the root of the problem. If the client is saying your company has a bad track record, don't argue. Arguing is a game you can't possibly win. It doesn't matter if the client is right or wrong; the important thing is to solve the problem.

Let's look in on our protagonists again:

Client: We called constantly. We asked for assistance, and nothing happened. Quite frankly, I don't even understand why we invited you here today.

Salesperson: Well, I have to tell you that I'm very concerned. And I certainly want to do something about this. What I suggest is this: I'll talk to my supervisor and review the whole relationship between our companies. And I'll be sure to mention everything you've said to me. And then I'll call you back, no later than tomorrow morning, and we'll discuss things and set up another meeting. Here's my card;

note that my number is 555-1212. You can always reach
me there, even if I'm out on a sales call. In the meantime,
if I could ask you for a favor, I'd appreciate it if you'd put
your recollections of how this situation arose in the form
of a memo to me so I can show it to my boss.

Note that the salesperson in this situation does several very important things:

1. He makes a concrete promise to the client: he will call her
    back tomorrow morning. It doesn't matter if the situation is
    resolved by then. The important thing is to reestablish a track
    record of promises kept to replace the one of promises bro-
    ken. By simply making the phone call tomorrow he can begin
    to rebuild his company's reliability.

2. He asks the client to take a specific step in reconstructing the
    relationship. The content of the step is less important than
    the action itself. Again, it's limited and specific. It doesn't re-
    quire any great leap of faith on the client's part. (A mistaken
    approach would be something along the lines of, "I'm just
    going to ask you to start trusting us again," a request that is
    not particularly justified at this point.)

Once these two things are accomplished, the salesperson
is going to have to work incrementally to rebuild the breached
trust between his company and the client. Under these circumstances, smaller promises are better than big, expansive ones.
Small promises can be kept easily, and with them you can move
the relationship forward.

FORWARD INTO
THE FUTURE

If you work this situation in the right way, you'll have reconstructed an extremely important relationship between your company and the client, one that can yield substantial rewards in the future. But it's not duty-free. This objection should teach you that the bond between you and your clients can be broken easily. What you need to do now is strengthen it.

You can do that in several ways:

1. *Make specific, deliverable promises.* Don't waste your time on airy generalities ("I'll work very hard to improve relationships between our two companies"). Instead, concentrate on achievable, recognizable goals ("I'll call you once a week for the next month, every Monday, to review where we stand").

2. *Increase face-time.* E-mail and even phone conversations can quickly turn impersonal. It's much better, whenever possible, to meet in person. That allows both of you to read one another's body language and expressions, which can do much more than words to cement a relationship.

3. *Create strong institutional ties.* The more you regularize your relationship with the client, the more powerful that bond. Find ways to make your contact with the customer regular and predictable—a phone call every fortnight at an agreed-upon time; e-mail exchanges on a schedule; once-a-month visits to iron out problems, and so on. If the customer knows that she can trust you to be responsive, she is more likely to trust you on the content of what you're delivering.

WHO MAKES THIS
OBJECTION?

No surprises here. Groups 1 and 4 are the most likely to bring up the bad track record barrier. Groups 2 and 3 may still raise the issue, but in their case the obstacle will be easier to overcome.

1. *Dominant.* This group, with its in-your-face mentality, has no hesitation telling you that you and your company have screwed up. In fact, when confronting people such as this your biggest challenge is going to be refraining from screaming back and slamming the door behind you as you exit. (Believe me, I've been guilty of this more than a few times.) With this group, you must distinguish between this objection as a negotiating tactic and as a genuine objection. Once you determine that the client really means it, he or she will respond to very specific acts on your part. Anything that smacks of vagueness will only serve to infuriate him or her.

2. *Influence.* These people don't like to think that you could be dishonest with them. The objection from them is going to come in a veiled form, often with a lot of qualification. "I'm not sure if you recognize . . .", "Perhaps you don't realize the impact of your decision to . . .", "You may not be aware, but . . ." To get them off this track, focus on the idea that you're *partners* in all of this. Both of you want what's best for their company; after all, if they're satisfied, they'll keep buying from you, and that's going to make you satisfied.

3. *Steadiness.* This group is the least likely to voice the objection about the bad track record, if only because they

despise confrontation, and this objection is a very confrontational one. Nonetheless, if they feel that your company has a bad record, they'll agonize about it and eventually bring it up. The best way to meet the objection is with concrete proposals. Don't spend a lot of emotional capital on them. They've got plenty of their own.

4. *Conscientious.* Perhaps the most likely to raise this objection, Conscientious people are perpetually dissatisfied with the service or product you're providing. So it's only natural that they look upon your relationship with a jaundiced eye. Everything seems to have gone wrong from the start. The whole thing has been nothing but problems. Why aren't you doing anything about it? With this group, it's especially important to move off the comments about the past and onto the promises for the future. Make very short-term commitments that you know you can fulfill easily and on time. Nothing else will rebuild their confidence.

WE'RE SWITCHING TO OVERSEAS VENDORS

10

A while ago I read a story, either in the newspaper or online, about a fast-food franchise that was considering outsourcing its drive-through window.

Yes, you read that right. When customers drove up to the window and a radio-distorted voice bawled, "Yes! May I interest you in our Mega-Maxi Million Calories Carb-Loaded Chocolate Pineapple Milkshake Burger with Extra Cheese today?" the voice would actually be coming from a call center in India, China, or another Eastern country. After some consideration, the company decided not to take this step, but it makes me wonder every time I hear a voice over a speaker if I'm really talking to someone residing in my time zone.

All of this isn't surprising. We live in a global economy. For the past 30 or 40 years, changes in communication, transportation, manufacturing, and information technology have been driving this connectedness, and right now there's very little that's manufactured solely in one country. We drive cars with spark plugs from Ohio, steering columns made in Ireland, tires from Jamaica, and electronics from Japan. All of which have been assembled at a plant in Ontario, Canada. If you think I'm joking, read through the driver's manual for your car very carefully and start doing some research on where its parts were made.

Thomas Friedman, the *New York Times* columnist, aptly summed it up in the title of his bestselling book: *The World Is Flat*. In other words, trade barriers are becoming increasingly obsolete, and today you're competing not just with other companies in the United States but with workers from around the globe.

So, it's not startling—or at least it shouldn't be—that the objection "We're switching to overseas vendors" is becoming more and more widespread. Nowadays it's easier to set up a deal with a manufacturer in another country and save on both wages and cost of goods.

WHY IS THE CLIENT DOING THIS?

As with most objections, your first priority should be to determine if this concern is a genuine one or a negotiating feint. Is the client *really* planning to switch to an overseas supplier? Or is this a way to get you to concede on price or delivery terms? Some judicious questioning can help decide which of these alternatives is true.

You can start by asking for the reasons behind the decision:

Salesperson: I see. Would you tell me the reasons for your decision to switch to overseas?

Client: We've found that the numbers work better for us.

Salesperson: Is it the manufacturing costs or the shipping that's an issue?

Client: Manufacturing. [*long pause*] But we could make a price concession there if we could get better delivery terms. If you can't give those to us, though, I'm afraid we're just going to have to go with our alternative in Bangladesh.

Salesperson: Let's discuss this in terms of the specific numbers involved.

In this situation the client was never very serious about going overseas. He just wanted to win some points on pricing. The salesperson chose to consider those points, but he could have stood firm and said, "I'm sorry, but I'm afraid we're not going to make that deal. You're better off going with your foreign vendor."

Now it's the client who's sweating. He doesn't want to have to go overseas. It's a pain in the neck—not to mention being potentially much more expensive than signing a domestic contract. Suddenly he discovers that there are obstacles to an overseas vendor. The objection is passed over, and the discussion resumes its normal course.

In discussions such as this, silence can be your friend. You want the client to do most of the talking anyway, and the more you stay silent, the more the client has a tendency to want to fill that silence by talking. By keeping quiet, you can learn some valuable information, and you can put subtle pressure on the client to tell you the real truth behind his objection.

Your decision about whether to make a concession or stand firm depends on your psychological reading of the client as well as how much research you've done about his or her company. These are among the questions you should investigate:

- Has this company employed foreign vendors in the past?

- Approximately what would it cost them in shipping? What would it cost in time to market lost?

- What would be the reaction of the client's customers if they knew that his company was purchasing materials from overseas?

- Is the company set up to make this shift in its suppliers? Do those companies have the necessary contacts and infrastructure?

All these questions should give you a good idea of how genuine this objection is.

Asking the Client the Hard Questions

One thing you'll quickly find as you probe deeper is that many clients haven't thought through what going with an overseas vendor will really mean. In your initial questions, there's no point in arguing with them. Let the facts speak for themselves:

Salesperson: Does that include the freight costs and insurance for overseas shipping?

Client: Yes, I believe it does.

Salesperson: What allowance do you make for intangibles?

Client: Such as what?

Here's where you've got a good opening. It seems, from this exchange, that the client hasn't fully thought through some of the consequences of going with an overseas vendor. You could follow up with:

Salesperson: Well, of course if you're shipping from overseas, there's always some uncertainty involved. There was a case a few years ago of a dock strike in San Francisco that tied up some products from Japan and China for a month. I'd sure hate to see something like that happen, but you know these things are uncertain. Then, of course, you have less control over what goes on abroad. Are you planning to send someone to inspect the factories where the product is made? You'll have to do that to conform with U.S. laws regarding the use of child labor abroad.

By this time, the client is probably wondering if there's any chance of getting the salesperson to start talking about a deal again.

When you start discussing imponderables such as the ones mentioned above with a client, it's a good idea to quantify them in dollars. That allows you to contrast them with the savings the customer will experience if she stays with you. You can estimate the amount of sales that will be lost while the client waits for a ship to unload at the dock, its cargo tangled in the bureaucratic nightmare of customs. Or you can suggest a dollar amount that will be necessary to cover the increased insurance on the product, not to mention freight and the ever-present uncertainty of foreign labor conditions.

MEETING THE OBJECTION HEAD-ON

If the objection is real, you can challenge it directly. Here are some bases on which to do so:

1. *Loyalty.* Sometimes it's also possible to appeal to clients on an emotional level—after all, they are breaking a long-standing bond with you. With certain types of customers (see below), it's worthwhile to make an appeal to their loyalty. You still have to

back up your appeal with facts, though. Is there a way you can quantify that loyalty? How much does it represent in dollars?

2. *Reliability.* Are the products manufactured overseas going to work as well as those made by your company? What about service? If a part breaks, how long will it take to get a replacement?

3. *Customer reaction.* In a postrecession economy many people don't like the idea of shipping jobs overseas. Is the client risking alienating her customers by switching to an overseas vendor?

4. *Speed to market.* How long will it take to get the parts from overseas? How will that impact the point at which the client's product hits the shelves? What overall effect will that have on the product's profitability and the client's revenue projections?

5. *Long-term relationships.* Is the client planning to build a long-term relationship with the overseas vendor? How easy will this be? What is the vendor's track record (as compared to yours)? How sure can the client be that the vendor will still be around in another couple of years?

All of these are good questions to ask the client to make her think about whether this is the best time to switch vendors. (As an additional point, you can mention that a period of economic malaise may not be the best time to take chances on a new vendor, especially one that's far away.)

WHEN THE CLIENT'S DETERMINED

If you can't get past the client's objection, avoid closing the door. I heard of a young salesman several years ago who, exasperated that his client was dropping him in favor of a vendor in China, stalked out of the room, slamming the door. The minute he got back to his desk, he sent a stinging e-mail to the client, accusing the VP of lying to him, betraying their friendship of five years, and doing everything but robbing church-going pregnant mothers. He sent copies of the e-mail to the VP's boss and to every other person he could think of at the company. Ah, he thought, revenge is sweet.

A year later, he saw, with great satisfaction, that the vendor the client had chosen over him had gone out of business. Smirking, he called up the VP. His pitch was singing through his head, along with the words "I told you so." He got four sentences into the call before the VP hung up on him.

No sale, no commission, no client.

In business, very few things are forever. Especially in the matter of different vendors, at a time when things are fluid and likely to continue so for the foreseeable future, it's essential to maintain good relationships. If the customer wants to drop you in favor of a cheaper vendor overseas, smile bravely, make sure she has your contact information, and call her regularly to ask if she's satisfied. You don't need to make a pitch for her coming back to you. Just ask her if the new vendor's product is solving her problems and leaving her satisfied. I'm assuming your product is better; if that's the case, time will bring the client back to you.

WHO MAKES THIS OBJECTION?

All four groups might make the objection to switch to an overseas vendor, but it may be phrased in somewhat different ways, depending on who's bringing it up.

1. *Dominant.* This group is more apt to raise this matter as a negotiating point. Even if they do bring it up as a serious possibility, you can take some comfort from the fact that they're going to be equally skeptical of an overseas vendor's product as they are of yours. As is usual with them, rely on facts and figures to show that by sticking with you they're getting a better deal. Emotional appeals will have little or no impact on them, but a focus on numbers will go a long way toward convincing them you're the right vendor.

2. *Influence.* Because this group is so focused on strong personal relationships, it's possible to pitch your argument around the fact that it's much easier to maintain strong ties with someone who's in the same time zone. Furthermore, having invested in building networking connections with you, they're less inclined than the Dominants to arbitrarily break those connections.

3. *Steadiness.* Switching vendors is a *big* decision, especially when it involves going with ones who are far removed and may not be responsive to the need for sudden changes and opportunities. Stress this point in your arguments with this group and you'll probably make a lot of progress. They don't like uncertainty, and because they don't like to make big decisions they'll be more inclined to stick with you as a known quantity.

4. *Conscientious.* This group may not be as excited by your product as you'd like them to be, but they're probably going to be equally unenthusiastic about what's dished up by your foreign competitors. They're susceptible to facts and figures—it's the cautious side of them—so you can use those to convince them that caution is the wiser course in this case.

YOU HAVE NOT OFFERED ME ONE REAL REASON TO BUY

11

Several times in my career—fortunately, not many—I've gone through sales pitches only to look at my audience halfway through and see them sitting on their hands. The vibe I've gotten from them isn't just halfhearted. It ranges from deeply unenthusiastic to actively hostile. In one particular case, I felt as if I were working a particularly tough crowd in a Vegas casino on a night when no one's been winning at the tables.

Any salesperson will tell you that the mood of your audience affects your presentation. That's true of sales just as it's true of acting. An actor whose performance on Broadway is greeted with yawns is going to find his energy level going down. Unless he can counter that, the next time he goes on stage it's likely that he'll give a less-inspired performance, leading to more ennui from the audience, and so on. It's a vicious cycle that ends with the actor finishing his career doing dinner theater for a retirement community in Miami Beach.

A sales presentation has a large acting component in it, and a salesperson is equally affected by the mood of her audience.

So you can imagine my feelings as I worked harder and harder to produce a positive reaction and got . . . nothing.

Finally, at the end of the presentation, the senior VP present straightened up in his chair, looked at me, and said, "Thanks for the pitch, Steve, but do you know, I listened very carefully, and you haven't given me one real reason to use your service."

Ouch!

WHAT'S *REALLY* BEING SAID?

This is a particularly tough objection to deal with because it seems to speak directly to your abilities as a salesperson. You find yourself frantically running over your pitch in your mind. Did I cover everything I was supposed to? Did I stress the unique elements of my product? Did I explain how my product will help solve an important problem for the company?

There are two things to keep in mind at this stage:

1. It's entirely possible—in fact, quite probable—that what you're seeing here is a negotiating tactic designed to put you on the defensive and score points for the client.

2. If the objection is genuine, it may not have much to do with you or your presentation. This sounds paradoxical, but I'll explain later. Right now, let's consider the first possibility.

Does He Really Mean It?

Did the VP really mean that he'd sat through my entire presentation—one that I'd thought out, tested, reviewed, and gone over time and time again—and in all that he hadn't found *one* reason to buy?

I concluded that this, in fact, was nonsense. Of course, he had reasons to buy. This wasn't about him struggling to figure out why he wanted my service. This was about him pushing against my pitch. So I took a deep breath and did what any good salesperson does.

I asked a question. I said, "Would you tell me what reasons to buy you were expecting from my presentation?"

There are two things about this kind of question. First, just that fact that you ask something instead of stating something is a bit startling to your audience. The VP was obviously anticipating pushback, preparing to answer me when I said, "You weren't listening? I gave you plenty of reasons to buy, but you're just not looking at them!" From there, with me on the ropes, he could push harder, convincing me (and the audience) that I was selling an inferior product that wasn't worth what I was asking. From that point, it was just a short step to pushing me down on price, on deliverables, on guarantees—in a word, on everything.

Instead, I did an end run around him. I asked a question that accomplished three important tasks:

1. It conveyed to him and to the rest of the assembled audience that I was genuinely interested in his opinion. It reestablished me as the primary initiator of the conversation and indicated that I was willing to listen to his opinion.

2. As a nonconfrontational question, it calmed the mood in the room. There are times when you're making a pitch or negotiating a deal when a superheated atmosphere can work to your advantage. [I discuss some of these times in my book *Negotiating Techniques (That Really Work!)*.] But at this point, I didn't want a confrontation. I wanted to continue the discussion.

3. By asking a question, I put the onus back on him to come up with a solution. Essentially, I told him to put up or shut up.

If he really had reasons to buy my product, I said—though not out loud—"Let's hear what they are." In effect, *I turned him into the pitchman for my product.*

And, in this case, sure enough: he did it. He enumerated three or four reasons to buy my service. The fact that he claimed I hadn't explained these in my presentation was beside the point. Just the fact that he'd now told me what he and his audience *wanted* to hear was enough for me to clinch the deal. I took his points, one by one, ran through them, expounded on them, and explained why my service would more than satisfy every one of them. By the end, I'd put him in a position where he *couldn't* refuse the deal I was offering. Because I'd just met every one of his reasons to buy.

What's Eating Him?

A long time ago, a very wise colleague of mine (well, okay, it was me) said, "If someone is upset or angry, chances are it isn't with you. It's probably something else in his or her life." The longer I'm around, the more true I've found that.

People get upset for all kinds of reasons, and most of them don't have anything to do with you. So when someone stands up and raises a very aggressive, confrontational objection, start by assuming that he or she isn't really angry about anything you've said or done. What's more likely is that there's something else in the background.

A couple of years ago, I started selling to a new client with a big office in New York. Just to get to him, I had to make my way through an army of gatekeepers across what felt like a football field of carpet and through a half dozen doors. I finally pene-trated to the inner sanctum and sat down in front of him, across a desk that looked and felt like a battleship.

Before I could even say a word, he started in on me. His face was red, he was yelling about all the damn salespeople who were hell-bent on wasting his time, and he didn't have time for any of them. This went on for four or five minutes, but from where I sat it seemed like four or five years. Part of me wanted to shrink down in my chair while the other (dominant) part wanted to stand up and tell him where he could stick his company, his of-fice, his desk, and himself.

Fortunately, I got control of my temper—not necessarily an easy thing. Rather than tell him off and end the call right there, I started asking questions, keeping my voice low and calm. I didn't respond to any provocation he offered, no matter how blatant. Slowly the atmosphere in the room changed. We moved from anger to conversation, and after of 15 or 20 minutes we were actually on a first-name basis. He ended up telling me that I was welcome to come back the following week and make another presentation to his senior staff, at which point he'd make a deci-sion whether or not to buy.

As I was leaving, his admin, who'd clearly been with him for some time and was looking very nervous, came up to me. "Mr. Schiffman," she said, "I hope you don't take anything Mr. [blank] said the wrong way. He's had a very hard time the past couple of weeks. His wife died after a long illness, and he's had to cope with his young children."

Suddenly it all made sense. And of course I reassured her that it was fine, that we'd talked and I was coming back the following week.

My lesson here is that there's very little reason on an initial sales call to yell. Sometimes we do it—I've been as guilty as anyone else over the years of losing my temper. But before we fly off the handle in retaliation against what seems an outrageous statement, stop and consider for a moment that the anger implied in the objection may not be directed against us.

WHO MAKES THIS OBJECTION?

At first glance, it's easy to see who is the most likely to make the objection that you have not offered a reason to buy. But in fact it may come from all four groups for different reasons.

1. *Dominant.* Both skeptical and aggressive, members of this group are most likely to raise this objection and to do so because they want to push back on your sales pitch. They're not going to take anything you've said as gospel. But with this group, something you should recognize is that, against all reason, sometimes *they want you to push back*. They don't respect someone who caves; they respect someone who argues. So if you're facing an audience of Dominants and someone says, "You haven't given us one good reason to buy," don't back off. Put the question back on that person: "What reasons do you expect?"

2. *Influence.* The objection when it comes from Influence types will be phrased in a much kinder fashion. Something along the lines of "But I don't see any clear reason yet for why I should buy from you." Or, "Don't you think you should explain to me why I should buy your product or service?" No matter that the question's phrasing is different. It's still the same issue. What these people are looking for are some specific reasons to buy.

3. *Steadiness.* People who belong to this group are apt to raise this objection when they're not entirely sure why they don't want to buy. Their caution sometimes leads them to miss the obvious benefits you're offering them. Confrontation with these people won't work—as it will with the Dominant group. Instead, they've got to be persuaded with facts and figures. One thing to keep in mind with this group (as well as Group 2) is that they're more inclined than others to keep their feelings bottled up, making them prone to this objection as a way of masking more complicated problems.

4. *Conscientious.* As you might expect, this is the other group for whom this is a common objection. Their lack of enthusiasm—very much what I encountered from the group I described at the beginning of this chapter—means that it's hard for them to spot the benefits your service is offering. As I indicated in the example, this is a case where you need to turn the tables back on them with questions. Find out the source of their concern, and address it.

YOUR PRODUCT OR SERVICE DOESN'T FIT IN WITH OUR COMPANY'S CULTURE

12

There's no question that it was a very different kind of company than she was used to selling to.

When the salesperson walked in the front door, she was greeted by the sight of two young men and a young woman racing through the lobby, waving Nerf guns, and yelling "Banzai!" at one another. On the walls were hanging a collection of random objects that looked as if they'd been looted from a pawn shop. She looked around, squared her shoulders, and asked the receptionist—who had green hair and two eyebrow piercings—to let the CEO know she was there for her appointment.

A few minutes later, she was introducing herself to a lanky young man in blue jeans and a tee shirt, with tattoos stretching from his wrist to his neck. They sat around his desk, heaped high with papers, stale donuts, and coffee cups. As they talked, he idly tossed darts at a board to which Warren Buffett's picture had been tacked.

She presented her case calmly and clearly. But at the end of her pitch, he swung his legs down from the desktop and said, "I'm sorry. But I don't think that kind of thing would go here. We're a free and easy kind of company, and you're way too button-down for us." His look made her conscious of her Armani suit, her three-inch heels, and her carefully coiffed head, with not a hair out of place.

CULTURE CLASH

Corporate America is changing—no question about it. When I started 35 years ago, most offices were run along the lines of the McMann and Tate Advertising Agency from the television show *Bewitched*. Everyone wore a suit and tie, pretty much everyone (except the secretary) was male, and there was a set protocol for how executives were treated by those below them.

Now things are different. "Business casual" has become standard in many companies, with the emphasis on casual. Suits and ties are used only for formal occasions, even though a lot of job applicants wear a suit and tie to their interviews. Employees express their individuality through the kinds of gewgaws they keep on their desks. And yes, there are some companies (especially on the West Coast) that encourage periodic Nerf fights between employees.

That said, there are also companies that remain the ultimate in button-down. A friend of mine recently related her experiences working for a leading investment firm in which there were rigid rules about who spoke to corporate officers, and even which staircase different levels of executives were allowed to travel on.

These are just some of the outward features of a culture. Along the same lines, a corporate culture will also play a role in determining how decisions are made, what kind of power leaders exercise and what form that takes, how decisions are made, and how the company and its employees determine their goals.

KNOW YOUR CULTURES

If, like the hapless salesperson in the story above, you've run into the objection that your product or service doesn't fit with the company's culture, you need to take a step back. Clearly you've made some assumptions about the company that are unwarranted. The biggest cause of this kind of mistake is a lack of adequate research.

I made the opening example very blatant to make a point, but sometimes the clash can be much more subtle. For instance, one type of corporate culture reserves decision making for the top echelons of the company. The remaining groups of executives and employees are charged with executing those decisions. For that reason, it's entirely possible for you to make a mistake not so much in what you're selling but in *whom* you're selling to. If your pitch is directed to lower- or mid-level managers, you may put them in the uncomfortable position of having to admit that they don't actually have the authority to make a decision as to whether to purchase your service.

No one likes to admit he or she lacks authority. Right there you've set up a potential source of hostility that can make this objection difficult to overcome.

The key is to study the culture of the company before you show up to sell to it. And the best place to start is the mission statement.

The concept of a mission statement has gone through waves of popularity; for a while everyone was writing and rewriting them, and then amid all the economic chaos of the past several years they've become less important. But if your target company has a mission statement, it can tell you something about the culture it's trying to achieve.

A company's culture refers to the organization's values, beliefs, and behavior it tries to encourage on the part of its employees. Sometimes this can be general and aspirational. For example, Google's mission statement when it was founded was "Don't be evil." The idea was that Google wanted to be a different kind of company from what it perceived the rest of corporate America as being. It would be a company that valued its employees and that provided a service that helped people live better lives. It would behave responsibly within its industry and do good socially as well as economically. I'll leave you to judge whether it has achieved that mission.

Another company with a strong mission statement is the Vermont-based ice cream company Ben & Jerry's. Founders Ben Cohen and Jerry Greenfield started their company in the late 1970s with the idea of concentrating on all-natural ingredients and giving back to the community—in this case, Burlington, Vermont. Although they have been bought out by the Unilever company and issues have come up about some of their contents, they still attempt to hold true to the original mission. Their statement is "We strive to make the best possible ice cream in the best way possible."

Don't Go Against the Culture

With all that in mind, what does this objection about the product or service not fitting in with corporate culture really come down to? What the young CEO who confronted our salesperson in the example above was really saying was, "You don't get us."

This isn't a frivolous objection. Trying to sell something to a group of clients when you don't understand them is an exercise in frustration on both sides. Think of Lady Gaga performing for a Mormon congregation in Salt Lake City and you'll get some idea of the possible disconnect.

But remember: you don't have to participate in the culture of the company you're selling to. You just have to understand it.

In addition to looking at the company's mission statement, it can help to understand the company's history and the history of its industry. For instance, the banking industry is generally a culturally conservative world. There are traditions on Wall Street that go back for many years and that instill the idea of staid respectability. On the other hand, the software industry, born in the innovative cityscapes of the Pacific Northwest (Microsoft) and Southern California (Apple), has little time for tradition. The software industry is one that constantly reinvents itself. "Tradition" in that industry is an insult, not something to aspire to.

So how do you overcome this objection, once it's raised?

You have to prove two things: first, you have to show that your service is infinitely adaptable; second, you have to show that it has integrity.

ADAPTABILITY AND INTEGRITY

What you should never do is try to change the company's culture to fit the product or service. That just sets up resistance and shows that you don't have knowledge of or respect for the company's mission Even if you're uncomfortable with the company's culture (and in the example I opened this chapter with, the salesperson was *way* outside her comfort zone), that's irrelevant to the central challenge at hand: selling your product or service.

Remember: *You don't have to work with them. You just have to sell to them.*

You should be reevaluating your product and thinking about how it furthers the company's mission and how it solves problems within the context of this corporate culture. You're fortunate because all companies are alike in certain important respects:

1. All companies want to make money.

2. All companies want to do so as efficiently as possible.

That means that the problems your service or product solves will be alike, no matter the company's culture. All that has to change is the style with which it solves those problems.

For instance, I sell the service of sales training. I've sold this to a lot of different companies with a lot of varying cultures, and in all cases the problem I've had to deal with is the same: salespeople, with all the will in the world, too often don't know how to sell.

In some companies, the culture is very much a top-down, hierarchy-conscious pyramid. At meetings of his top executives the CEO emerges from his office to issue instructions. Contact with him is limited and formalized. Everyone in the pyramid knows precisely what her or his role and responsibility is and how far she or he can go in making decisions. In such situations, my presentations are very formal, and I stress the responsibility of salespeople to report upward to their supervisors. I give my presentation, the sales force asks questions, we run through some exercises, and then they're dismissed.

On the other hand, I've trained at companies where the relationship between executives and employees is a much more level playing field. In one case, the CEO actually had a cubicle, as did his employees, and referred to himself as a "janitor" rather than an officer of the company. Everyone called him by his first name, and employees weren't shy about coming up to him and offering their opinion about the latest corporate decision. In such a company, top-down training doesn't make sense. It just makes the employees angry. Here, my training sessions were more about working things out as a group: criticizing one another's strengths and weaknesses and then discussing collectively how to improve them. The CEO himself took an active and enthusiastic part in these discussions.

I don't want to suggest that either of these two cultures is superior to the other. Both achieve significant results for their companies' bottom lines. The point is, you can't present your services to the companies in the same way. You have to adapt to the culture and deal with it, regardless of which you personally favor.

In circumstances such as the one with which I started out this chapter, I'd pull back hard and attempt to reschedule the sales call. Trying to completely change style in the middle of a presentation risks making you look like an opportunist who believes in nothing. Better to let a few weeks go by until the unfortunate impression of your first attempt has faded a bit.

WHO MAKES THIS OBJECTION?

Any of the four groups we've been considering can raise the point about the product or service not fitting in with the corporate culture, because any company culture includes elements of these groups. Nonetheless, some are more prone to raise the point than others.

1. *Dominant.* These people tend to prefer a loose organizational structure and thus a culture that operates from the bottom up rather than the reverse. Their inherent skepticism and constant questioning of authority makes them disinclined to hierarchical structures. When some of them wind up in such a company, they generally make themselves and everyone around them miserable by their constant questioning. As managers, they'll raise this objection with you often if they think you're too rigid and formal to fit in with their preferred anarchic structure.

2. *Influence.* Because of their focus on networks and interaction, these people function best in a flat structure. They like being able to walk around and talk to one another, no matter what level of the company they're at. People like this can be a powerful force in helping a flat structure to work because in such an organization information is the grease that keeps all the wheels moving smoothly. Influence people aren't hoarders of information; quite the contrary. They like to see it widely distributed. They'll object, like the Dominants, to anything that smacks of a pyramid or that discourages mingling among employees.

3. *Steadiness.* People in this group are born followers. As such, they prefer a highly structured culture, one in which they're told what to do and can do it. Their discomfort with decision making is offset in such a culture by the tendency of others to make decisions for them. Thus, if your product or service requires them to exercise a lot of autonomy, they're likely to object that it's not a good fit.

4. *Conscientious.* These people can work in either a flat organization or one that's more structured. They bring elements

that are conducive to both: the skepticism that's the lifeblood of a flat organization and the caution in which the preference is for others to make choices from the top down. In the end, their tendency to dislike change may lead them to question your product or service from a cultural standpoint. After all, it's not precisely what they're used to.

I CANNOT GET DELIVERY WHEN I NEED IT

13

I swear the following story is true.

A publishing company in New York had contracted an author in Canada to write a book on a really quick deadline. The author struggled, worked at night, put his marriage in jeopardy, and finished the book just under the wire.

A month or so after he'd completed the manuscript and sent it off, he began to wonder where the check was for the last half of his advance. He started calling the publisher. The folks there told him the check was in the mail. He waited two weeks, but it didn't show up. He called again. They told him, with considerable embarrassment, that the paperwork had been lost and that this time the check really *was* in the mail. He waited another two weeks.

Nothing.

Now steam was coming out of his ears. He called again. Sorry, said the publisher, there was a mistake on our part. The check is in the mail, and we're sending you a present along with it to make up for this snafu.

Slightly mollified, the author went back to waiting. A week later the check finally showed up, unaccompanied by any present.

Two weeks after that, he received a call from the Canadian customs authority. They said he had a package waiting if he'd care to come pick it up.

He drove down to the station and picked it up. It turned out that the publisher, in an effort to compensate the author for his time and irritation, had sent a basket of gourmet sausages and cheese. Unfortunately, the package had been held up at the Canadian border, and by the time it arrived in his city, the cheese was moldy and the sausages had gone bad.

So the author had his check—finally—along with a basket of moldy cheese and rotten sausage.

I tell you this story to show how easy it is for something to go wrong with delivery. There are an enormous number of variables, and any one of them can steer into a ditch and throw off the whole chain. When a client starts telling you that he or she needs faster delivery than you're promising, it's time to stop and think. After all, unlike an objection concerning price, this is something you may not have much control over. Whereas *you* set the price, delivery involves external forces: shipping, the state of the roads, or, if the product is coming from overseas, such possible events as a storm and dock worker strikes.

THE VARIABLES INVOLVED

Nonetheless, speeded-up delivery may be something you can offer. The question is, is that *really* what the client wants? And what's he or she willing to give up for it?

In many respects, this chapter is a corollary of Chapter 1, about pricing. Delivery is simply another side of pricing.

You need to start a conversation, which should bring out some of the following points:

- Who is the end customer for the product?

- What has been the average delivery time in the past?

- Are there competing firms that can provide a faster delivery time?

- What are the implications for your client if delivery is not made in the time frame requested?

The answers to all of these questions give you ammunition for negotiations. They're essential to overcoming this objection about not getting delivery on time.

Once you've accumulated the information, you can steer the conversation around to the clients' most important considerations. For example:

Client: I'm concerned you can't deliver when we need the product.

Salesperson: You mentioned earlier that in the past you've had a faster fulfillment time from us. Is that right?

Client: Yes. We expect the product in our warehouses three weeks from when the order is placed.

Salesperson: I see. And as I understand it, your reason for choosing us is that we're able to deliver faster than firms X, Y, and Z. Correct?

Client: Right. But now if you're going to take five weeks to fulfill orders, we'll have to reconsider that.

Salesperson: Would you tell me, are there particular times of the year when quicker delivery is essential?

Client: I'd say during the holiday season, from October through the end of December, is when it's most important.

Salesperson: If we were able to speed up fulfillment time during those months, could you accept a longer delivery time, say, from February through June?

Client: Yes, we could do that if there was a price break per unit for those orders that take longer to fulfill.

Salesperson: So would you tell me what's more important during the holiday season: price or how fast we can move the product into your warehouse?

Client: I'd say delivery time is paramount.

With all this information, you've got a framework to negotiate. You have some idea—and in real life you'd probably want to accumulate much more information than this—of what kind of schedule the client needs, when she needs it, and the relative balance between pricing and delivery.

Notice in the previous exchange that the salesperson restates the client's point several times, asking for confirmation. This is known as mirrored questioning, and it's a useful technique. It confirms information and firmly commits both parties to it. It also keeps pushing the conversational burden back to the client, where it should be. Remember, in general the client should be doing about 80 percent of the talking to your 20 percent.

NEVER SOMETHING FOR NOTHING

Notice as well that the salesperson phrases each stage of the conversation in terms of a trade-off: speeded-up delivery implies a higher unit price. Just as we saw earlier in the discussion about discounting, there's no reason to give the client something for nothing. Every part of the transaction you hold in your hands is important capital, and you don't want to give it away. Instead, establish what the client is willing to trade off and at what price. In the previous example, you can see that the delivery objection is valid only for certain times of the year. During winter and early spring, delivery time is less important than pricing. You can propose extending delivery time in return for a lower per-unit price. On the other hand, during the peak holiday season the client may be willing to pay more to ensure faster fulfillment.

Don't let the conversation get bogged down in what you provided the client in the past. You should know that information, but it's not a useful conversational topic. All that it's going to lead to is a series of tortured explanations or recriminations, none of which will get you to the sale.

DON'T OVERPROMISE

This seems like a good time to talk about one of the commandments of selling: *thou shalt not overpromise to the client.*

In my years, I've heard countless horror stories of salespeople who, in their eagerness to clinch a sale, made commitments to the client that they couldn't possibly keep. One salesperson I know in his early years on the job proudly marched into his office with the news that he'd signed one of the biggest deals in the firm's history. His boss reviewed the paperwork and then, calling the salesperson into his office, pointed out that the terms he'd agreed to meant that their company would lose money over the next year of the contract and that the amount they'd make over the following year was so small as to be practically nonexistent. The matter went all the way up the line to the vice president, and shortly afterward the salesperson was told to clean out his desk.

It's true, as I've said on many occasions, that the purpose of negotiations is to get the client to say yes. But that's only half the battle. The client has to say yes in a way that meets your needs as well as his. In short, both of you have to come out of the discussion a winner.

Going back to the scenario I outlined previously: it would be all too easy for the salesperson to say something along the lines of, "Oh, I know in the past we managed delivery in four weeks. That'll be no problem going forward." But it very well *could* be a problem if Production or some other part of the company isn't able to meet that aggressive deadline. Before you promise something to a client, make sure it's a promise you can keep. This means that often the best thing you can say is, "I'll get back to you on that." You need to collect the information about what your client wants, take it back to your company, and discuss the best way to approach it. It may take more time, but it's preferable to signing a hastily conceived agreement and finding out when you return to the office that you'll have to call the client back and explain why you can't keep to the terms you just agreed to.

Avoiding Overpromising

Overpromising is a sin much committed by younger salespeople who are anxious to settle terms and who want to please the client. Experienced negotiators may use this sort of thing against you, suggesting that if you don't agree to their requested terms immediately, they'll be forced to turn elsewhere.

This is another instance where doing research beforehand will pay off. You should have a clear idea before going on your sales call what the other possible sources of products and services for the client are and what they're priced at. That way, when the client says, "Well, if you can't agree to this proposal here and now, I'm going to call Corporation ABC and sign with them," you can reply, "You can certainly do that, but I think you'll find that even though their delivery time is a week better than ours, their unit price is $.20 higher, and they have significant quality control issues that still haven't been resolved. Wouldn't it be better to let me discuss this with others in my office and get back to you in the next few days? Let's set a time to talk right now. I think that's a better way to proceed, don't you?"

Again, this throws the matter back on the client and offers a specific time to resolve the issue. It also lets him know that you're aware of his alternative to a negotiated agreement and that he won't benefit by simply walking away from you.

Which leads me to the last point here: ultimately your greatest power in any sale when confronted by an objection is your ability to walk away from it. In my book *Negotiation Techniques (That Really Work!)*, I've discussed the concept of the *alternative to an agreement*; essentially, this is the cost to you of not making the sale to the client. If it's going to cost you $3,000 per month to keep your products in the warehouse, and the client's best proposal to you is $2,500, it's going to be cheaper for you not to do the deal. (This idea was explored by Roger Fisher and William Ury in their 1981 book *Getting to Yes: Negotiating Without Giving In*. They refer to the concept as best alternative to a negotiated agreement, or BATNA. As I've also explained in my book on negotiations, I think the concept is overblown by many salespeople, but it can be useful if done right.)

Just remember that making a bad sale is much worse than making no sale. The consequences of making a bad sale will follow you wherever you go; making no sale just means you move on to the next sales call and get to work.

WHO MAKES THIS OBJECTION?

The way the objection to not getting delivery on time is posed is very similar to the way the pricing objection is raised.

1. *Dominant.* Customers from this group will raise this objection as part of a flurry of challenges to you. They're not going to take anything on faith, and the real trick is to get them to slow down enough to discuss what they really want and what's important to them. The problem with them isn't that they don't want to take 80 percent of the conversation; it's that they want to dominate *100 percent.* Keep your sentences short and punchy and loaded with facts and figures. That's the kind of thing they respond to best.

2. *Influence.* These customers are just as forceful as the Dominant group, but they want to keep bringing the conversation back to you. For this reason, they're the most likely to try to keep it focused on what the delivery schedule was in the past and to try to get you to agree to recommit to that. As networkers, they want to establish a close connection to you. That's fine up to a point, but keep the conversation on the point, rather than letting it go wandering into side channels. You need to find out what *they* want, not the other way around.

3. *Steadiness.* You'll need to keep pushing these people because it's so hard to drag an opinion out of them. Patience is your biggest ally here. Keep coming back over and over again to the issue of their needs. Make it clear to them that you're there to help them solve a problem.

4. *Conscientious.* This is the group to whom it's often easy to overpromise because they're so unresponsive. As they sit,

with blank faces, you can find yourself struggling to get a reaction from them by proposing better and better terms. They'll question everything that you bring up. *Why* can't you go back to the old delivery schedule? *Why* isn't your production department up to getting the product out earlier? Why, why, why? Pump them full of raw data and stick to your guns. Their level of enthusiasm doesn't matter as long as you can get them to the point of agreement.

I CAN GET THE PRODUCT SOMEWHERE ELSE

14

Interviewed about the Marx Brothers movie *Monkey Business,* the great Groucho Marx said, "Everyone believes he's an individual, and everyone else is nothing." *Monkey Business* expresses this idea better than has ever been done before (or since, in my opinion) on film. But the same might be said of products and services.

Every product and service wants to be unique. Whatever makes it different is sometimes termed its Unique Selling Proposition (USP). Jack Trout wrote a bestselling book about this topic 10 years ago titled *Differentiate or Die: Survival in Our Era of Killer Competition.*

One of your most powerful tools as a salesperson is the conviction that what you're selling represents a unique solution to a problem. There will be many other products or services that address the problem, but only one—yours—will solve it in this way. So when you meet this objection, your natural tendency may be to think that you and your company have failed. Clearly someone has duplicated what you're doing, and you'll have to turn around and go back to the office, tail between your legs.

I had an experience like this several years ago. I called on a midsized company, laid out my sales force training program to the executives assembled in a conference room, and sat back, waiting for questions. I have to admit I was pretty complacent, since I'd been doing this for enough years to think I could anticipate anything they were likely to throw at me.

The CEO leaned across the table and said, "Thanks, Steve, but I hope you appreciate that you're not offering us anything here that we can't get somewhere else."

I was floored. It had been years since I'd run into this sort of thing. I prided myself on the fact that my approach to sales training is different from anything else out there (as I hope you'll realize, having read this far in my book). I fought down momentary panic and asked him to clarify what he meant.

He smiled patronizingly. "I mean, there are a lot of sales training programs out there. You want a premium price to teach us something we can get at half the cost—and it's just the same old thing."

One part of me wanted to slam my hand down on the table and shout, "Dammit, it's *not* the same old thing!" But a more rational part of my brain kicked in. If all he was getting at was that I was offering the same tired nostrums that his salespeople had heard a hundred times before, clearly I was doing an inadequate job explaining my program. And it was up to me, after all, and no one else, to fix the situation.

"TELL ME ABOUT WHAT I SAID"

I took a few moments to regroup and rethink my strategy. Then I said something along the lines of, "Well, that's a bit surprising to me, since I believe my approach to the problems of selling is unique and will lead to results that can't be duplicated by any other program. Perhaps you could explain to me, based on the presentation I've just given, what you think the main tenets of my sales system are?"

This approach had two advantages. First, by putting the ball back in his court it gave me some time to think. Second, it made me listen to what he thought I'd said.

This is a useful exercise and worth going through. It's like the old game of Telephone that they used to play at kids' parties when I was young. You all sit in a circle. One person whispers a sentence to the kid on his right. The kid whispers it to the next kid on her right, and so on around the circle until it gets back to the originator of the sentence. The game is to see how much the sentence has changed from its original form.

In the same way, if the CEO had misunderstood or misheard what I'd presented, it would go on being misrepresented all the way down the line of his direct reports, their reports, and the reports' reports. To avoid that kind of misunderstanding, it was essential that he and I communicate clearly with each other from the beginning.

In this case, the CEO gave a two-minute summation of the Schiffman method of sales training. By the time he finished, I had thought through my approach. I'd also listened carefully to what he'd said and picked out the places where I'd fallen down in my communication.

"Thanks," I said. "But I don't think I explained myself very clearly. Here's how it works."

This time when I went through my sales training program, I stopped every couple of minutes to illustrate how it differed from the competition. I also prefaced these sections by saying, "Here's why my approach works better, and here are the benefits it will bring to your company." When I got to the end, the CEO thought about things and then said, "Well, that makes it a lot clearer.

We'll need to review this approach, but it seems as if it could make a lot of sense for us." I was able to start breathing again. The sale was back on track.

CLEAR COMMUNICATION: THE KEY TO SALES

So far in this book I've focused most of my attention on the importance of listening to what the client is saying. That's because in my experience this is where most salespeople are deficient: they talk when they should listen.

But there's another skill, equally important, that's key to making any sale. You've got to be able to communicate about the product you're selling. It's surprising how many salespeople have a problem with this. Then again, I suppose it's not that surprising, since there's no sales school you can go to in order to learn this stuff.

What does good communication consist of? Basically it all comes down to these four elements:

1. *Clear thinking.* Many years ago, my piano teacher, Mrs. Pulaski, used to tell me, "Steve, before you go out and play a piece for an audience, you have to know it *twice as well* as you're going to play it." At the time, like most 10-year-olds, I thought she was exaggerating. Now, with the wisdom of years, I realize she knew what she was talking about. (Thanks, Mrs. Pulaski, wherever you are!) When you set out to explain a product or a service to a single client or to an audience of many people, assume that the strain of the moment is going to make you forget things or mix them up a bit. But the better you know your product, the more comfortable you are with its ins and

outs, advantages and difficulties, the better impression you'll make on your audience.

2. *Straightforward language.* If you ever want to hear an example of how *not* to explain something, I invite you to sit down with a manual of instructions written by someone in the government. It doesn't matter if you're a Democrat or a Republican, conservative or liberal, young or old. I guarantee you'll only understand a third of what's being said. That's because so many of these manuals are written in "governmentese," a kind of weird semilanguage that's designed to obfuscate and confuse. To avoid this kind of thing, there are a couple of simple rules to follow:

- Use simple words rather than long words. You're not trying to impress your audience with your vocabulary or your education; you're trying to convince them to buy something.

- Avoid jargon and the kind of alphabet-soup acronyms that are especially prevalent in the computer software business.

- Use the active voice rather than the passive. You'll find your presentation is punchier and has compressed more information into a shorter period of time.

- Repeat any important points at least twice during the presentation.

- The beginning and the end are strategically the most important parts of the presentation and receive the most attention from the audience. Highlight your most important information by putting it there.

3. *Logical order.* In the trial scene in *Alice in Wonderland*, a court official is about to read a piece of evidence to the king. "Where shall I begin, Your Majesty?" he asks. "Begin at the beginning," replies the king, "and go on until you come to the end. Then stop." This is a sound piece of advice. Every presentation has a compelling, logical order in which the information should be presented. Figure it out beforehand and stick to it. That way you'll be less likely to leave out an important piece of information, and you'll impress the client with your organization and clearheadedness—qualities they hope will be reflected in the efficacy of what you're selling.

4. *Stop.* Too many salespeople, having made all the points they need to make about what they're selling, feel compelled to go on making them over and over again until the client is ready to throw something at them. Before you arrive to give your presentation, you should know exactly how long has been allotted. Respect your audience's time, and stick to the schedule. Be sure to allow adequate time for questions and discussion.

PUTTING IT ALL TOGETHER: YOUR UNIQUE SELLING PROPOSITION

Following these rules, you should have a clear, compelling presentation ready for the client. In it, you'll stress the way in which what you're selling will solve a problem; you'll explain specifically which features of the product or service will offer benefits to the client; you'll quantify, as much as possible, these benefits in dollars and cents; and finally—and in some ways most important—you'll explain, point by point, how what you're selling is different from everything else on the market.

This, as I remarked on earlier, is sometimes called your Unique Selling Proposition. It's the most important way you can anticipate and preempt the objection that "I can get this product somewhere else." Remember, though, it's not enough just to *say* your product is better; you've got to show it. That means digging into facts and figures that prove to the client that your product will provide advantages that go beyond what else is out there. It also means knowing your competition and spending some time going over in your own mind the Unique Selling Proposition that their sales force is pushing. After all, just because you think what you're selling is the best, don't you think your competitors think the same thing? Of course they do. But the more you can get inside their heads and figure out what they're promising, the better positioned you are to make sure what you're selling is clearly the best alternative for the client.

WHO MAKES THIS OBJECTION?

As I hope I've made clear, if you structure your presentation correctly and think through both your own USP and that of your competition, the objection that the product or service can be obtained somewhere else, ideally, shouldn't come up. That said, when the objection is raised—and it will be—the way you counteract it will vary somewhat depending on which of our four groups brings it up.

1. *Dominant.* This group prides itself on its knowledge and its willingness to challenge you and not take anything for granted. They'll pepper your presentation with questions, assertions, and requests for more information. If ever there was a time when you have to know your material twice or

even three times as well as you think necessary, it's when presenting to this group. The good news is that of the four groups they're probably the most responsive to a strong, knowledgeable presentation, backed up with a lot of data.

2. *Influence.* Don't let their friendliness fool you; these people aren't about to buy from you if they think your product is easily available somewhere else. And because of their networking skills, they know all about what the competition's offering and how much it costs. It's particularly important to stay in touch with this group in between sales calls. You can even ask them for help in the process of formulating your USP. Ask them how they'd see the product solving problems for them and what features they'd like to see in it.

3. *Steadiness.* Their lack of assertiveness makes them, in some ways, less likely than the other three to raise this objection. However, it can be a tool they use in their desire to avoid making a decision. For this reason, you must be prepared to enumerate, one by one, the special features of what you're selling and to dismiss, point by point, their complaint that "this sounds just like Product X sold by the ABC Company."

4. *Conscientious.* Data, data, data. That's the way to beat this group. Don't expect to carry them along on a wave of emotion and enthusiasm; that's not going to happen. But if you can show them just why your product fills a unique niche in the market, they'll get behind it, even without an apparent show of emotion.

I NEED TO THINK
ABOUT IT

It's the ultimate nondecision decision. And it drives you around
the bend.

I don't think there's a salesperson alive who hasn't at some
point heard this kind of thing. You're pitching; you're in the groove.
You've got the audience, and you know that you're hitting every
point with them. You're winding up for the final delivery, the
one that's going to blow them away. You throw the pitch, and
then . . . and then . . .

"Let me think about it."

There's nothing that can drain the energy out of a room faster
than this objection. Mainly because it seems so unanswerable.
You've been taught—not least by me—that pushing against the
client just tends to generate resistance and in the long run will
lose you the sale. You can't overcome someone who is bound and
determined to put off making a decision. The effect is to emotionally slow you down to the point that it's almost impossible to
rebuild your energy.

EMOTIONAL VAMPIRES

I'm not a big believer in the supernatural. If my house is haunted,
I don't know about it. I've spent enough time walking down

lonely dark streets in Manhattan—where I live—to cure me of believing in ghosts. But there's one thing my years in sales have taught me to believe in: vampires.

That's right. Vampires.

Oh, all right. Not the Bela Lugosi/Christopher Lee/Dracula kind. Not the ones who appear in tuxedos and suck the blood out of beautiful girls in diaphanous gowns at midnight. But there are vampires. Trust me about this.

There are vampires who can suck the energy right out of a sales meeting.

About 10 years ago, I was sitting in such a meeting. I wasn't the presenter; I was there to offer support. As such, I was in an interesting position to observe what happened. The salesperson went in, guns blazing, and gave his presentation. It went well; I could see that. His audience was impressed. He had the command of facts and fingers at his fingertips. He was doing the right thing, asking questions of his audience, getting them to talk, observing the 80/20 rule (letting his audience do 80 percent of the talking while he did 20 percent of the questioning). He believed in what he was selling, and he motivated the audience to do so, too.

I was impressed as he moved in for the kill.

And then it happened. The vampire.

One guy in the back raised his hand for a question. The salesperson, full of confidence and hubris, called on him. The guy said, "Well . . ." He let the word hang in the air for what seemed like five minutes. Then he said, "It's very *interesting*." The word *interesting* sounded like a tropical disease.

He cleared his throat and said, "We'll need to . . . consider it."

You could feel—I mean, actually *feel*—the energy disappearing. What had been a decision suddenly became a question. It suddenly became a concern. Then suddenly a postponement.

And then it was over. We all sat back and felt the weight of time pressing down on us as we waited for the salesperson to respond. I don't need to tell you the end of the story. Needless to say, the sale vanished like a shadow in the bright morning sun. And I was left to ponder the question of *why*.

IT'S ALL ABOUT TIMING

Being a salesperson is like being an actor. It's all about timing. And about presenting and selling an image.

This isn't to say it's fake. The best selling, like the best acting, is very genuine. But a lot of selling is involved with presentation: finding the right pitch, the right presentation, the right tone that can hold your story together.

That means that it involves energy. Before they go on stage, actors do some energy-building exercises. They get together in a back room of the theater and start jogging in place together. They run back and forth, jump up and down, and do other, even stranger, exercises to build up their energy for that brief moment when they'll be on stage, when they'll have to convey to the audience, through word and gesture, a wide range of emotion.

If they do it right, and if the mood holds, they can sell the story to the audience. If not, coughing breaks out, the viewers move restlessly back and forth, and the next morning the reviewers search for alternative phrases to "stinks."

In the same way, a salesperson has to find a way to get over the energy vampires in her or his audience, to revitalize a group that has had the rug pulled out from under it by the "Let me think about it" objection.

Having seen this happen many times, I've evolved some safety measures to counteract this particular energy-draining objection:

1. *Meet the objection head-on.* The natural tendency of most salespeople is to either avoid the objection by not dealing with it or try to find a way around it. All of this, though, misses the central point: The power of this objection is that it puts off making a decision. That's precisely what you *don't* want to do. So push the decision. Insist that there isn't room for dithering; there has to be a decision right here and now. Anything else is unacceptable.

2. *Call out the objector.* Sometimes it's not enough to push for a decision against the nondecider; you have to specifically call out the person who's the energy vampire. In one case, when I encountered someone who sat through my presentation with folded arms and who finished it with, "Well, I'll have to think about it," I lost my temper. (Okay, maybe having a four-hour drive to this sales call compounded things.) I snapped, "You can think about it all you want, but that's not going to change any of the numbers! Either you want the service or you don't!" There were a few moments of uncomfortable silence, and then the executive laughed and said, "All right, let's do this." The whole tone of the meeting turned around, and the energy drain vanished.

3. *Be specific.* Nothing disarms an emotional vampire more than a focus on details, because once you start bringing the discussion down to concrete issues of facts, dates, and commitments, it's much harder for the objector to maintain a pose of disinterest. So rather than take a confrontational approach, as I did in the example above, sidestep the objection and move the discussion to a different level. Say something like, "While you're considering this, let me just emphasize the following four points." Offer up the figures for projected revenue in the first two years that the client will realize by purchasing your

product or service. Facts and figures are your stake and holy water in your quest to vanquish sales vampires.

WHEN THE OBJECTION IS GENUINE

Most of the time, the aforementioned approaches will disarm the objection to "think about it." However, it's possible that it is merely an excuse on the part of the executive to end the discussion and get you out the door. She may simply say, "I appreciate your time, but I really do need to think about it. And now, I've got another meeting."

You need to be sensitive to this kind of thing. Planting yourself firmly in the conference room and refusing to give up any ground isn't going to get you anything if the executive really wants to take the time to think things over. All you'll do is annoy her and botch any chance of a sale at a future date.

On the other hand, you don't want to just leave things hanging. Out of sight, out of mind is nowhere more true than in sales. Once you've gone through that door, the executive has a thousand things to occupy her mind, and most of them are more important than you and what you're selling. So you need to keep the door propped open.

If you judge that the objection is being raised because the executive genuinely wants to think about things a bit more, *set a time for a second sales call*. I can't emphasize this point enough. You *must* take the initiative to ask for another appointment. Say something like, "Well, I can certainly understand the need to consider this fully. I'd like to take up this discussion again next week. I'll make another appointment with your administrative assistant on the way out, and you and I can continue our conversation at that time."

Once you've made the appointment, compile more material to support your case and send it to the client. Keep her focused on what problems will be solved by your offering. If the appointment you've made is more than a week away, try to schedule a short, five-minute phone call in the interim to discuss the new material you've sent. (You need to find a level of being aggressive in your sales pitch that stops just short of being annoying.)

When you return for your second appointment, lead with something like, "Now that you've had an opportunity to consider fully what I said to you in our last meeting, I'm confident you'll see the value of what I'm presenting to you." Assume that the executive has fully studied the materials you've sent and that she's been able to consult others in her organization and come to a firm conclusion to buy what you're selling. This is an instance where a strong, positive approach can work miracles.

WHO MAKES THIS OBJECTION?

In general, some of the four groups aren't inclined to bring up the need to think about it. But one group in particular has this one as its default sales objection.

1. *Dominant.* Members of this group are too strong-minded and forceful to be inclined toward this objection. If anything, their tendency is to make a decision very quickly, sometimes before you've had a chance to fully develop your pitch. If you've analyzed your audience and it's made up of Dominants, this objection may take you by surprise. You'd be wise to assume, though, that it's a negotiating tactic and come back strongly to counter it. The Dominant, having tested your resolve, will quickly move in another direction.

2. *Influence.* Networkers who want to like you and want to be liked will sometimes raise this objection to avoid an outright rejection. They don't like to do anything that will cut you off from further contact. However, you need to make clear that you're just as interested as they are in maintaining a long-term relationship, whether they make a buy from you this time or not. You can get them off this particular objection by stressing the importance of making a decision *now* and not putting it off indefinitely, while at the same time stressing that you'll be coming back in the future with other sales pitches.

3. *Steadiness.* As you might expect from a group that hates to make decisions, members of this type often employ this objection. They just don't want to do anything that rocks the boat—including anything they haven't done before. But you're asking them to make a change, and that makes them nervous. So they put off doing anything by asking for more time to consider. Here's where you've got to push the hardest, relying on your mastery of the details of your product, focusing on its specific benefits. The struggle to overcome this group's tendency toward vampirism can be a severe one—but with persistence you can win it.

4. *Conscientious.* Don't mistake their lack of enthusiasm for a lack of interest or involvement. Members of this group are masters of detail, but unlike Dominants, they don't incline toward a rush to judgment. For this reason, this group may make this objection as a genuine consideration—they really do need some more time to think, to consult, and to examine all the facts and figures. Attempts to rush them are going to be counterproductive. Instead, give them the space they need to arrive at a decision they are happy with.

YOU HAVEN'T BEEN HONEST WITH ME

A couple of years ago, a friend of mine started dating again after a long hiatus. Soon he met a woman with whom he enjoyed spending time. They started by going to a concert together and progressed to dinners, walks in Central Park, and visits to clubs. It all seemed to be going very well. When I saw my friend, he was head over heels about this woman. She was all he could talk about. I checked my mail every day, waiting for the announcement of an engagement or a wedding.

One day, not having seen my friend for several weeks, I ran into him in the street. He looked tired and older, and his face was drawn in a permanent scowl. We chatted for a few moments, and then I asked about his girlfriend.

He shook his head. "Don't talk to me about her!" he growled.

I was practically bowled over with astonishment. After a few minutes, I managed to guide him into a nearby restaurant where, over the course of a couple of drinks, I wormed the story out of him.

It seems that while he'd been seeing this woman, he'd also maintained a very close platonic friendship with another female, someone he'd known for several years. That wouldn't have been a problem, probably, but he somehow neglected to tell his girl-friend of this woman's existence. In fact, not to put too fine a point on it, he carefully concealed it from her by whatever means were necessary.

You can see where this is leading. He got careless one day, and his girlfriend found out. They had a confrontation that started with bitter words and angry questions and escalated to mutual screaming. Finally she threw the clincher at him: "You haven't been honest with me!"

He couldn't answer that—though he tried. Because, as he now admitted to me and to himself, he hadn't. He'd lied by omission, and as he must have known in the back of his mind it would, sooner or later it came back to bite him.

RESPECT THE OTHER PARTY

In truth, as I've said elsewhere, everybody lies. Sometimes we do so for what we think are excellent motives, sometimes we convince ourselves that it's necessary (for example, in the case of my friend), and sometimes we do it consciously to gain an advantage.

I'd like to tell you to be like George Washington, the Father of Our Country, and never tell lies when you're selling. But I know that somewhere along the line you're probably going to do it, even if it's unintentional. So my advice to you is threefold:

1. Keep the lying to a minimum.

2. Never lie to try to gain an advantage over the client.

3. If you're caught out in a fib, have enough respect for the client to admit it and work to rebuild the trust between you.

Let's consider these points.

Little White Lies

Remember the last time you and your spouse were on the way out the door to a party? Perhaps your wife asked, "Does this dress make me look fat?" Or your husband asked, "Is my bald spot noticeable?" Did you tell the truth?

Most of us have grown into the habit of telling "little white lies" over the years. I call them "Grandma lies" because they're the kind of thing you tell Grandma if you don't want to hurt her feelings. Sure, she may have left the Christmas cake in the oven for too long and forgotten to put two eggs in the batter. But she's your grandmother—you don't want to make her upset. So you tell a little lie. You tell her what she wants to hear.

This sort of lie is very common in sales, because salespeople have a natural tendency to want to please the client. After all, if the client's happy, chances are that we'll be able to wrap up the sale.

The danger lies in *telling the clients what they want to hear, rather than giving the truth*. For example:

Client: When can I expect delivery of the first 5,000 units?

Salesperson: We can do that by June 1.

Client: That's no good. I need those units in the warehouse by mid-May. Can you move that delivery date up?

Salesperson: Sure. May 15 is no problem at all.

Well, yes, there *is* a problem. In this instance, the salesperson has made a promise without checking back with her home office. Is the May 15 date possible? Maybe. But if it's not, she's already made a commitment to the client, one that it'll be hard to take back. And when the units don't show up at the warehouse on May 15, her credibility with the client will suffer.

The salesperson succumbed to the fatal temptation of Grandma lying. The client wanted something, so she said it was no problem to bump up the delivery date. In fact, the best course would have been to ask herself some questions:

- Why does the client need the product earlier?

- What is the client willing to give up in order to get the product earlier?

- What are the consequences of the product not arriving by May 15?

These questions provide a framework of information with which the salesperson can go back to her office and put together a counteroffer, one that's workable.

If, during the aforementioned conversation, the client said something like, "Well, I need a decision right now!" the salesperson can reply, "I'm sorry, but those sorts of questions always have to be referred to Mr. X, and he's out of the office today. I'll have to get back to you tomorrow."

This is an example of what, to me, is an acceptable fib. It's a bit like the last time you bought a car. The salesperson made an offer, you countered with another price, and the salesperson, with a huge sigh, got up and said, "Well, I'll have to go talk to my manager about this."

I can guarantee you that when he went back and spent 10 minutes in the manager's office, about two of those minutes were actually spent talking about your offer. But having told a little fib—that he had to get this whole deal cleared first—he had to follow up. That sort of fibbing is okay; it doesn't hurt anyone and doesn't seriously damage trust. But keep it to a minimum.

Never Tell a Big Lie to the Client

Imagine, if you will, the following scenario:

A salesperson calls on a prospect and tells him that the salesperson's company can provide 50,000 widgets over the next year, half of them deliverable in a month. In return for this speedy delivery date, he asks for an increased price of $0.10 per widget. The customer hems and haws a bit, but the salesperson informs him that this increased cost is necessary to cover the increased manufacturing costs that will be incurred when production is speeded up to meet the next month's deadline.

After more hemming and hawing, the customer agrees to the higher price on the first 25,000 widgets and signs the paperwork.

A week later, the customer discovers that the company represented by the salesperson had an overstock of 30,000 widgets from a canceled order the previous month. These widgets were sitting in the warehouse collecting dust. All the company now had to do was ship them to the customer—at a premium price.

Seething, the prospect calls the salesperson, cancels the order, and declares his intention of never doing business with the company again.

A sad case, but not necessarily uncommon. Even if the customer didn't find out about what the salesperson had pulled right away, he probably would have found out sooner or later. The results would have been the same. Trust broken, future orders canceled, and a client lost.

The salesperson might have argued in his defense that his lie was a small one (that the higher price was needed to cover manufacturing costs) and that the price *was* needed to cover the cost of the previously canceled order. He might be able to convince himself with this sort of logic, but it doesn't matter to the customer. All the client cares about is the end result as far as he's concerned. In this case, the salesperson lied, and he'll probably do it again. So no more sales from that rep.

The lesson: don't lie to gain an advantage. The client will find out, and you'll see that there's hell to pay.

Admit to an Error

Nobody likes owning up to doing something wrong. But the consequences of covering up can be much worse. (Remember Nixon and Watergate?) I've got good reason to know this.

At one point earlier in my career I contacted a client with whom I'd set up a training session. I asked to change the date of the session, explaining that I'd be out of town on personal business that day, something I'd forgotten about when I set up the session. She graciously agreed, and we hung up.

I was surprised when I got to the session to find that she greeted me coldly and was obviously irritated with me. After the session ended, she came up, seething. She informed me that she'd called my office the day of the originally scheduled session and was informed by my administrative assistant that I was in town, giving a seminar at another company. What, she demanded, did I think I was doing?

I had to swallow a few times before answering. One part of me felt like getting defensive and starting to raise my voice in anger. Why should I have to justify myself to her?

Then good sense kicked in. I said, "You're absolutely right. It was a big mistake on my part. I'd previously scheduled this other session, and when I realized I was double-booked I was embarrassed and made the 'personal business' excuse to you. It was the wrong thing for me to do, and I hope you can forgive me and look past it. I promise it won't happen again."

It would be nice to say that she forgave me and everything was fine. In fact, it took a little while and some more groveling on my part. But in the end, I retained her company as a client and gradually rebuilt her level of trust in me.

If you're caught out in a fib, even one that you don't think is very important, don't try to justify it. That's not what the client wants to hear. Apologize, promise not to do it again, and move on. (That's a pretty good rule for life as well as for sales, by the way.)

WHO MAKES THIS OBJECTION?

Obviously all four of our groups can and will make this objection about dishonesty if you lie to them and they realize it. But each one's approach will be different.

1. *Dominant.* These people, because they're aggressive by nature, are going to get up in your face if they find you have lied. They're naturally skeptical as well, so they're not likely to accept at face value your apologies or explanations. Take your time, and don't start fighting with them about whether what you did was right. It will probably take a long while to smooth things over with them, so be patient.

2. *Influence.* This group is inclined to like you, which makes it harder for them when they perceive that they've been betrayed. They have a stronger emotional reaction than the other groups to acts of treachery—and they'll see it that way—because it impinges on their whole worldview. Work

with them closely, making sure at every step that they're aware of your reasoning, and you can win them around again.

3. *Steadiness.* This group, of the four, will probably be the most reluctant to directly challenge you. However, that doesn't mean you have free rein to lie to them. They're going to remain aware of any breach of trust; they just won't bring it up directly. You may have to probe and pry in order to get it out of them. But a simple, direct apology for any untruths and a promise to be completely honest in future will go a long way.

4. *Conscientious.* This group can be completely unnerving when they make this objection because in all probability they'll just sit there and stare at you, waiting for you to react. Talking to them can be like hitting a wet sponge. You just sink into it without any reaction. Precisely for this reason it's going to take quite a while for you to be sure that they're comfortable with you—in fact, you may never be quite sure. All the more reason to avoid lying to them (or to any other client) as much as possible.

I'M GETTING OUT OF THE BUSINESS YOUR PRODUCT OR SERVICE IS AIMED AT

All the objections I've discussed so far in this book have been ones that you can get over or around or under. Some of them require some fancy footwork on your part, but none of them is insurmountable.

But what do you do when a client tells you that she doesn't need your product or service anymore? That her company is going into another kind of business? This situation can be especially heartbreaking if it happens to an established client, one on whom you've counted for strong sales for years.

This objection illustrates something that frustrates me about many salespeople, especially in difficult times. *They're too willing to give up.*

I don't expect you to overcome every difficulty and make a sale. Sometimes you work and work, and it just doesn't happen. If we could wave a magic wand and make every objection disappear, I wouldn't be writing this book; I'd be retired in my beach house in Waikiki getting a suntan. Sadly, life doesn't work like that.

The art of selling is, to a large extent, about recognizing opportunities and knowing how to take advantage of them. And that's what too few salespeople do on a consistent basis. When a client tells them that the company is changing to another product line or shifting its production procedures in such a way as to make what the salesperson is selling obsolete or unnecessary, they give up. If they'd just persist, they'd find a whole new crop of opportunities.

INFORMATION, PLEASE

Let me give you an example of how to handle this in a much more productive manner. Imagine that you're talking to a client with whom you've been dealing for several years. And suddenly he gives you the devastating news.

Client: I'm sorry to tell you this, but we won't be needing your service anymore.

Salesperson: What do you mean?

Client: Well, we're shifting production to move away from the Widget-maker 2000. We've found that we can cut costs and maintain a high quality of widgets if we shift to a WidgetPro 800. So I'm sorry to say that your maintenance services for the Widget-maker 2000 aren't going to be necessary after next month.

Salesperson: I see. Would you explain a bit more what the advantages are of moving to the WidgetPro 800?

Client: It'll be able to produce 10 percent more widgets per hour, and we won't have to increase our headcount to cover that. Also, the widgets will have some features that we believe our customers will be attracted to.

Salesperson: What service contract are you going to sign for it?

Client: We're considering going with Company X; they have expertise in servicing the WidgetPro line.

Salesperson: Will the transition be immediate next month?

Client: Um, no, we'll make the shift over several months.

Salesperson: But during those transition months, the Widget-makers will still need servicing, won't they? Why not continue your contract with us, but on a revised basis, for that period? In fact, I think I can show you how to use your existing Widget-makers to work in tandem with the new machinery, which would increase your production by up to 15 percent an hour.

Client: Really? Well, if you come in with a plan for that, we'll have something to talk about.

Salesperson: Excellent! Let's set up another meeting in a few weeks to discuss this further. What's a good day and time for you?

The method that the salesperson in this conversation is using should come as no surprise to you. If you want to sell, you need information. In this case, the salesperson wants to know something about the client's overall goal—which, it turns out, is to increase production without increasing headcount. From this point, the salesperson has to determine what he can sell that will help solve the client's problem.

The salesperson doesn't make any attempt to change the client's mind about shifting to the new machinery. It's highly unlikely that he could persuade the client to stick with the old system, and in any case the decision to change may well have been made by someone substantially above the client's level in the organization. Rather, the salesperson wants to offer a benefit and develop a chance to continue the conversation. Hence the final question, trying to nail down a time for the next meeting.

As long as a conversation is going on, the sale isn't dead.

THERE ARE OTHER PARTS
OF THE COMPANY

In the previous example, I've assumed that you want to continue to sell to the same part of the company and to sell more or less the same product. But don't overlook the fact that there are many other parts of the company, and some of them may be interested in buying from you.

As you develop a relationship with individuals in any company, it's important to see them not just as a source of sales but as conduits of information. Call them every few weeks to chat and, among other things, find out how the company is doing. You don't have to ask for specific numbers—in any case, they won't give them to you. But you can certainly inquire about any rumors that the company may be shifting its priorities, changing the products it manufactures, or substantially revising its procedures in a way that will impact your sales. In this way, when your client tells you that she or he can no longer buy from you because your product isn't relevant anymore, the news won't come as a shock to you.

In fact, use the opportunity to ask about other areas of the company that might need what you're selling. I'm assuming you've built up a good track record with this client and that she or he is willing to give you some names of other people in the company you should talk to. Write down the names and follow up with them as soon as possible. Be sure to ask if you can give the name of the person who recommended them. That way you can start the conversation with something like, "Hi, Ms. Prospect? Steve Schiffman here. Mr. Client recommended I speak with you about a service that I provide, one that he's used for a number of years. I wonder if we could set up a time to discuss this in detail. Is there a date and time that works best for you?"

"IS THERE SOMETHING WE CAN DO FOR YOU IN THE FUTURE?"

One more thing to remember in this situation: nothing is forever. Even if the client's company is shifting into another line of business or making changes that no longer require what you're selling, it's important to retain that client as a prospect. Things change, after all; for example:

- The company may find that the new line of business is not as lucrative as it thought and shift back.

- The company may discover that it has a need for what you're selling after all.

- The company may be acquired by a larger company that needs the product or service you're selling.

- Your own company may increase its offerings to include a product or service that the client will want.

All these possibilities show that whatever you do, don't close any doors. If a client's account is going away—even if it's the big one you were counting on to make your quota—accept the situation with grace and establish a regular communication with the client. You can say something like, "Well, I certainly understand you making this shift. But we've had such a great relationship that I don't want to lose touch. How about if I call you on the fifth of every month and we'll talk about how things are going? I'd really appreciate any insights you can give me about the evolution of the industry."

Here you're being specific about how you want to stay in touch and at the same time complimenting the client on his or her knowledge of the industry—everybody succumbs to a little flattery.

WHO MAKES THIS OBJECTION?

All four groups will make this objection about getting out of the business that the product or service is aimed at. In this instance there's not a huge amount of difference in the way they'll make the objection to you. However, you'll find it easier to deal with some of the groups than with others.

1. *Dominant.* The biggest problem with these people is getting past their attempts to cut off the discussion. Once they've told you that your product or service is no longer relevant to their business, they have a hard time seeing that there's anything more for you to say. After all, runs their reasoning, the company is shifting to a different set of suppliers, so what's the point of continuing the discussion? You need to muster all of your patience and explain carefully that you'd like to stay in touch and that there may be some alternatives. As much as possible, be specific

about what those alternatives are; Dominant people don't respond well to generalities.

2. *Influence.* These people are the easiest to deal with in the case of this objection because they *want* to stay in touch with you. They've already got a big network of former business acquaintances and partners with whom they stay in touch, and they're eager to add you to the list. Call regularly; these people are a valuable source of information not only about their own company but about the industry as a whole (since they've got contacts throughout it).

3. *Steadiness.* It's going to be much harder than the Influence group to talk to a Steadiness group or individual about this objection. Their reluctance to commit to anything makes it difficult for them to see the importance of looking at alternatives. When they're confronted with several possible ways in which your product or service could be of use, they usually waver. But facts—cold, hard facts—are your best friends here. With some persistence, you can win them over.

4. *Conscientious.* For this group, the bad news is just one more item. Since they're unenthusiastic and reserved, they won't make a big effort to stay in touch with you. In fact, their skepticism pushes them away, since you no longer seem to be of any use. But they'll yield to facts, even if they don't get excited about them.

IF I BUY IT, I'LL LOSE MY JOB!

This is a pretty shocking objection to run into, one that can really throw you for a loop.

A couple of years ago, a salesperson I know made a presentation that he was convinced was completely irresistible. He had all the statistics at his fingertips and could cite chapter and verse about the benefits of the product. He'd made this same presentation a half dozen times before, and it had always resulted in a sale—in several cases setting records for his company.

And then . . .

You guessed it. After the presentation, the manager stood up, thanked him, and politely showed him the door. The salesperson was so flabbergasted that he'd failed that he couldn't think of a thing to say until he was actually opening the door to his car in the parking lot.

He turned around and marched back into the building, up the elevator, and past the startled administrative assistant into the office.

"Look," he said, "would you tell me what the problem is? You're the first person in weeks who hasn't been interested."

The manager looked quickly around the room and stood up. "Come on," he said. "Let's talk about it over a drink."

Fifteen minutes later, sitting in a secluded booth at a nearby restaurant, the manager leaned toward the salesperson and said, "Here's the deal. If I buy this product, I'll be out of a job."

THE FEAR-BASED OBJECTION

The fear-based objection plays upon the salesperson's natural sympathy with the person she or he is talking to. After all, you're both professionals, you both need to earn a living, and neither of you wants to make things difficult for the other. It's only natural that when the manager says, "I'll be out of a job if I make this deal," your first instinct is to back off.

"This guy must have the boss from hell!" you think. "The poor guy probably is hanging on by a thread, and I'm not going to be the person who snaps it."

In fact, as we'll see when we start examining it closely, this objection is not only a nonobjection—it's a great starting-off point for numerous opportunities. The way to look at this objection is as a kind of prompt. It tells you that it's time to start asking questions.

We'll assume for the moment that the fear expressed by the manager is real. (There's also the fake fear-based objection, which we'll get to later.) The guy is genuinely concerned that if he accepts your offer and purchases your product, his job will be in peril. So your *first* priority is to find out why.

There could be several reasons:

1. The company could be in a relationship with a competing vendor, one in which the CEO or another higher-up has a strong personal stake.

2. The company could be involved in delicate negotiations that preclude any deal like the one you are suggesting.

3. The manager himself or herself could be the problem. Perhaps the manager is on probation for having made one too many bad deals in the past and can't close a sale on his or her own.

Let's go through these various scenarios.

The Company Is in a Relationship with a Competing Vendor

It's possible that at some point the company has entered into a relationship with one of your competitors, a relationship that it's reluctant to break. There could be a lot of reasons for this, but your job is to find out if there's a sound financial reason. To deal with this, think about asking the following questions:

- "Is the competitor's product or service better than yours?"

- "Is it cheaper?"

- "Are the terms of delivery and service better?"

- "Does the contract with your competitor preclude any other bids?"

- "Does the competitor have an extra-business relationship with a member of upper management?"

If the answer to the latter question is yes, you'll need to probe a bit and find out what the nature of that relationship is. That will tell you if it's even possible for you to overcome this objection and make the sale.

As well, it will determine your next move. If the competitor has a strong personal relationship with a member of upper management, it's time for you to move your pitch from the manager to the upper ranks of the company where the decision to buy will be made. You can suggest to the manager that you understand her or his dilemma and perhaps it would be better if you spoke directly to the CEO (or CFO, CMO, COO, or whomever) and laid out the reasons why your product or service is the better way to go. In all likelihood, the manager will be grateful that the matter is being taken off her or his plate.

The Company Is in Delicate Negotiations

It's possible that at this point the company is involved in an activity that precludes the possibility of making a deal with you. This is particularly applicable if the firm is in the process of being bought by someone else. If that's the case, keep two things in mind:

> *First*, the manager won't tell you about it; there are very strict rules about revealing information about mergers and acquisitions.
>
> *Second*, the sale isn't lost, only delayed.

Sometimes the research you do on a company should tell you about these things in advance and warn you that you may run into some form of this objection. After all, we live in an information age where it's hard to keep much of anything secret. If the company is on the verge of being bought, you'll probably know about it. However, sometimes these things do stay hush hush, and there's nothing you can do to make a sale—at least a big sale—in the final stages of this process. Just relax, maintain the contact, and come back later when the dust has settled.

The Manager Is in Trouble

This is a tough one, because it's very hard for the manager to talk about it. After all, no one wants to admit that she or he screwed up. The trick in such a situation is to remove the source of anxiety.

If the manager is reluctant to make the deal and is voicing her objection in such apocalyptic terms, it's important to understand what the problem was with her previous deals. Did she pay too much? Did she agree to long-term arrangements that were unfavorable to the company? Did she purchase what proved to be an unreliable or unsafe product?

Your questioning here has to be discreet and delicate. Here's one way to approach it:

Salesperson: I certainly don't want to put your job in jeopardy. I wonder, though, if you would explain to me if the problem is with the product itself.

Manager: Well . . . no. The product is fine. We've bought widgets like this in the past.

Salesperson: Yes, in fact from my company. So then, is the problem with the size of the order I suggested? Because that's open to discussion.

Manager: No, no, the size of the order is fine. I'm more concerned about the . . . well, your asking price is pretty high.

Salesperson: I see. So there's a problem with price. Is this a problem you've had before with us?

Manager: To tell you the truth, yes. I don't want to get in trouble again for making a deal of this importance that's at a price we just can't support.

Salesperson: Okay. I understand that and, as I say, I don't think *either* of us benefits from a deal that's not favorable to *both* of us. So let's discuss price versus delivery time and unit features . . .

At this point, the discussion becomes focused where it should be: on *what's being sold*. And that's where deals are made.

THE FAKE OBJECTION

Up to this point I've been dealing with this objection as a genuine one. The manager really is worried about losing his job if he accepts your offer. But this kind of objection can also be used as a gambit by skilled negotiators. And you've got to watch out for that.

A lot of the ability to detect a fake objection comes down to reading body language and voice. Someone who's throwing out this objection as a way of pushing you off your stride is going to be confident, aggressive, and assertive. These are some of the signs to look for:

- Erect posture, head upright, jaw set

- Arms crossed

- Legs crossed

- Leaning forward

- Voice loud

This body language, combined with this objection, really means, "Oh, come on! You don't expect me to go for that pitch, do you? Make me a *real* offer."

This sort of strong negotiating stance is going to call for an equally strong posture on your part. You can counter with your own set of aggressive signals and hold to your own terms, or you can seek to find some common ground where a deal can be worked out. It's possible from the "I could lose my job" objection that you're pretty far apart on your negotiating stance. However, it's equally possible that this is simply the client's opening move, attempting to push you back from your proposal and sap your confidence. In either case, my prescription is the same: start by trying to find out where the problem is. Ask questions about each aspect of the product or service. Then invite the client to make a counteroffer. This is a particularly useful tactic, because it puts the ball back in their court and gets the conversation off the objection and onto the much better track of "So what would it take for you to accept this sale?" Once the talk has been worked around to this point, you stand a good chance of landing the deal.

WHO MAKES THIS OBJECTION?

Each of our four groups is likely to make the "I could lose my job" objection, but for somewhat different reasons.

1. *Dominant.* This group is most likely to raise this point as a false objection. After all, they are the ones who are the most aggressive, and the most skeptical. They don't believe that you're offering the best deal, so they come at you with a powerful objection that can push you back and force you to regroup. Push back, though, and they're likely to yield to your logic.

2. *Influence.* Their penchant for networking gives them special knowledge that may be denied to others in the company. If there's a special reason why a deal can't be made at

this time, they're more likely to know about it than any of
the other groups of customers. But they also want to help
you solve your problem, so they're inclined to meet you
more than halfway as you try to figure out how to overcome this objection.

3. *Steadiness.* As a group that's probably more cautious than
   any of the other three, these are the people most inclined
   toward this objection. They're perpetually glancing over
   their shoulder to make sure no one's standing there with
   an ax. For this reason, a large part of your pitch has to be
   devoted to assuring them that this is the right decision—
   above all, that it's *safe*. Your presentation should minimize
   the risks both to the company and to the individuals' own
   careers. If you've identified a client or a group of clients as
   belonging to this category, you can be sure that when they
   raise this objection it's born of a genuine fear. Your job is to
   allay that fear and to help them make a positive decision.

4. *Conscientious.* This group, though they are never inclined
   to be enthusiastic, can be won over by very specific facts and
   figures. Their very pessimism inclines them toward this objection because they can always see the downside to every
   proposal. At the same time, their quest for hard data plays
   into your hands. As long as you come with plenty of information designed to back up your claims for the product or
   service, you can convince this group to go along with you.

WE ARE HAPPY WITH OUR CURRENT VENDOR

I was making a round of cold calls recently, pushing my way through a list of prospects. As usual, some were more responsive than others, but on the whole I was feeling good about my day.

And then I hit it: the objection that's like a brick wall.

The executive listened to my pitch all the way through, with barely a question. Then he cleared his throat and said, "I'm sorry you've wasted your time—and mine. We're very happy with our current vendor. Good-bye."

Click!

PICK YOURSELF UP

It's never easy to find any silver lining when you run into such a flat-out rejection. One approach, of course, simply is to move on to the next call and put it out of your mind. But I don't like to give up without a fight, and something in the smug tone of the voice on the other end of the line got my dander up. I paced up and down my office for a bit to cool off, and then I called him back.

Politely, I asked Mr. So-and-So whether he would mind if we talked further about his happiness regarding the current vendor.

Seeming taken aback that I had the nerve to call him again, he agreed.

So I started to probe. How often did his current vendor supply training for his sales force? What were the main features of the training? What follow-up did they offer? How easy was it to reach them if a question came up? And so on. I kept asking question after question until finally he said, "Steve, I'm puzzled as to why you want all this information."

"It's simple," I told him. "You said you're happy with the service that's being provided to you. So that raises two points to me: first, I want to know as much about that service as possible so I can offer you the same service *or better;* second, I want to find out if perhaps you're not happy with the vendor but you don't know it yet."

There was a long pause at the end of the line, and then he said, "Well, I can understand your first point, and I appreciate it. But don't you think if I were unhappy about something like this that I'd know it?"

I said, "Sometimes. But other times people are unhappy but aren't aware of it. Let me show you."

Silence on the line. I took that as consent.

"You said earlier that your current vendor offers training once a year, right?"

He agreed.

"Do you think that's enough?"

"For my company, sure," he said.

"Do you know how often your competition is training their sales force?"

He had to admit he didn't.

I named two of his main competitors and said, "Both of these companies offer three training seminars a year. They do a big seminar in the spring and then two smaller ones four months apart. Then they have a short review session right before the onset of the holiday season. That way their sales force is energized and recommitted to their mission and ready to go right before the most important period of the year."

I let him think that over for a minute. Then I said, "So. Still happy with your current vendor?"

I won't give you the details of how the conversation continued. You can use your imagination. In the end, he agreed to consider my offer and ask his current vendor if they could match it. They couldn't, and I landed the contract. All because I wasn't willing to give up and because I asked the right questions.

NOTHING'S EVER PERFECT

For most clients, telling you they're satisfied with their current vendor is a polite way of saying, "I'm really busy right now and don't want to waste time talking to you. Don't bore me with details, because I've already made up my mind that I don't want what you're selling."

For these people, the key is persistence, as it is with most objections. That's because in truth people are never fully satisfied with what they've got.

Rather than stopping when you hit this particular brick wall, do what I always advise: start asking questions. As you do so, there are some important rules to follow:

1. *Don't make assumptions.* Don't assume because the client says he's satisfied with his current vendor that he is, in fact, really satisfied. He may be unhappy but just not know it yet.

2. *Focus on the facts.* Any good reporter will tell you that a news story follows the basic structure of *who, what, where, when,* and *why.* Your job is to assemble as many facts as possible about what the current vendor is providing.

3. *Look for the problem to be solved.* The customer is buying from her or his current vendor because what they're selling solves a problem. If it didn't solve the problem, the customer wouldn't keep buying it. So find out what problem the customer wants to solve and how her or his vendor is solving it.

4. *Figure out how your product or service can solve the problem better.* This is the whole key to overcoming this objection and making the sale. You need to prove to the prospect that what you're selling can fix the problem better than anything sold by anyone else. (If you don't believe that, you need to get into another line of work because, as I always say, believing in yourself and what you sell is the one of the chief Schiffman commandments of sales.)

5. *Look for clues.* Sometimes a prospect's dissatisfaction can be indicated by nothing more than a pause or an odd turn of phrase. Be alert for these kinds of clues; they'll give you a valuable opening.

Let's look at how this might work:

Prospect: I don't want to take up any more of your time. We're happy with the vendor we're using right now.

Salesperson: I understand, but believe me, I've got plenty of time to talk. I wonder if I could just ask you a couple of quick questions.

Prospect: Okay.

Salesperson: How long have you been using your vendor?

Prospect: About 10 years.

Salesperson: Have you been provided with timely delivery in those years?

Prospect: Uh . . . yeah.

Salesperson: Does that include the holiday season?

Prospect: Well, everyone's a little behind during the holidays.

Salesperson: I see.

(*Note*: Here's the clue. But the salesperson doesn't need to jump on it with both feet just yet. Rather, she concentrates on gathering some more information.)

Salesperson: I wonder if you would tell me about a time when the vendor was late during the holidays. It's a pretty busy time, as you say.

Prospect: Well, last Christmas season, we didn't receive shipment until the week before Christmas. That was a bit tough because we missed the sales in the period right after Thanksgiving. But I think everyone was having a rough time because of the weather problems in the eastern part of the country.

Salesperson: Yes, I remember. We had to struggle, but with some good organization and determination we made all our deliveries on time.

Prospect: Really?

Salesperson: Absolutely.

(*Note*: Now the seed has been planted in the prospect's mind.)

Salesperson: Was this the only time you had that problem?

Prospect: There were some issues in the spring, but those got resolved.

Salesperson: I'm glad to hear it. Did they cost you money?

Prospect: Well, a bit. Fortunately we were able to deal with them before it got serious.

Salesperson: That's good.

(*Note*: Now comes the pitch.)

Salesperson: To my company, nothing is more important than maintaining our on-time deliveries to our customers. In fact, we're able to guarantee those deliveries, and if for any reason we miss one, we offer a 10 percent discount on the next order to make up for the lost revenue.

Of course, the salesperson could have made that pitch right at the beginning. But the prospect wasn't in the mood to hear it then. All he wanted to do was get off the phone. Now, as a result of a series of questions, he's ready to think in terms of dollars and cents about how much his current vendor is costing him in lost sales opportunities.

It's important to make the prospect aware that significant money is involved, even if the loss isn't a direct one. These are some possibilities:

- The current vendor is costing the prospect time—and time, as we all know, is money.

- The current vendor's product or service presents a risk to the prospect that could translate into lost dollars or higher insurance premiums.

- Technological weaknesses in the current vendor's product are resulting in the prospect falling behind the industry leaders, resulting in lost sales and lost revenue.

- The current vendor's delivery schedule means it's impossible for the prospect to take advantage of certain market opportunities that would have resulted in significant sales.

It's your job to make this case to the prospect, to make her or him realize that you're talking about dollars and cents. That's why you have to frame your comments as specifically as possible.

DO YOUR RESEARCH

All of this won't come without some preparation. It's an axiom of mine that a salesperson ought to know a client's business at least as well as, if not better than, the client knows it. In the case of a prospect, before you call you need to get a sense of the scope of the company, something of its history, and its chief officers and their relationship to one another on the company's organization chart. You also need to have an idea of who the prospect's customers are, who her or his chief vendors are, and if there's any history of difficulties with the latter. Keeping all this information readily available where you can access it during the call will help make you invulnerable to this objection.

WHO MAKES THIS OBJECTION?

As with most of the objections in this book, the one about being happy with the current vendor can be offered by any of the four groups we've been considering. But some are unlikely to raise it as a serious point. Instead, you'll probably hear about it from the others.

1. *Dominant.* The Dominants always want to impress you with their assertiveness and power. They are also questioning and skeptical, so it's quite possible they'll bring up this objection. If you've determined that the person or group of people you're talking to falls into this group, be careful when this objection comes up. They like to test you, and this may be a test to see if you'll back down at the first sign of opposition. As long as you're ready with facts and figures and don't show an indication of being easily intimidated, they'll remove their objections when you confront them with the facts.

2. *Influence.* They don't want to limit the number of people with whom they develop a professional relationship. This is both an advantage and a disadvantage for you, since often people who belong to this group may try to use their networking skills to avoid making a clear commitment to what you're selling. However, in the case of this objection it means they're less likely than the other three to raise it.

3. *Steadiness.* One thing this group doesn't like—change. They're the most conservative of the four groups, resisting anything that requires them to develop new procedures or a new way of thinking. For this reason, they're the most likely to raise this objection and to cling to it like a drowning

person holding on to a life preserver. You'll really have to work to extract from them what they don't find good about their current vendor relationship. Your best bet is a steady, patient stream of questions. Don't be aggressive or bad-mouth their current vendor (not really a good idea in any case) because that will just stir up resistance.

4. *Conscientious.* They may not be happy with their vendor at the moment, but that doesn't mean they're going to switch to you. They'll pepper you with questions, pushing you away and implying, quite possibly, that none of you— your company or the current vendor—really understands their situation. Trying to rally their enthusiasm is a losing proposition because they don't have any. What they *do* have is a clear commitment to the bottom line. So rely on your facts and figures, and you'll be home-free.

WE DON'T NEED ANY AT THIS TIME

There's a crispness in the air on early fall days that seems to bring out the business side in most of us. During the summer I've found that on sales calls everything seems more laid back and peaceful. The client and I will chat about our lives, our children (and in my case, grandchildren), sports teams, and so on. But when the weather starts to turn colder and the leaves change from green to yellow and red, suddenly the conversations pick up speed. At that point, everything is sharp and to the point.

That was the case on a call I made several years ago. It was in late September, and looking out my window I could see the brilliant orange foliage of a tree and a stretch of bright blue sky beyond. I went through my pitch for my sales force training program, asking questions and getting short, sharp answers from the prospect. Even though I tried to do less talking, the call felt like a presentation rather than a conversation. I slowed down the pace a bit, but it was no use. I got to the end and asked if there were any questions.

"Nope," he said. And then came the cutoff line. "I'm sorry, but we don't need any at this time."

GET BACK ON THE HORSE

At this point, the easiest thing for me to do would have been to say, "Okay, thanks for your time," and hang up the phone. I had other calls to make (if you don't make at least five cold calls a day, you need to think about doing something other than sales for a living). There wasn't all that much at stake in this call, and I could easily move along and forget about it.

But one of my principles kept kicking me in the back of the head, preventing me from setting down the phone. That principle is this: *a blocked sale is an opportunity.*

What I mean by that is that when a salesperson runs into an objection, he or she can do one of two things: find a way around the objection—which I've been showing you how to do in the preceding chapters—or find a way of continuing the sale on other terms. I couldn't think of a way around the "I don't need any of what you're selling right now" objection, but that just meant I had to find a way of changing the terms of the discussion.

I took a deep breath and plunged in. "I appreciate your candor," I said. "I wonder, though, if I could ask you a couple more questions." Without waiting for a response (a response might have given the prospect the opportunity to tell me he didn't have time to continue talking), I asked, "When was the last time your sales force received systematic training?"

His response hinted at underlying uncertainty. "A month ago?" he said, as though it were a question.

"I see. Would you tell me who did the training?"

He named one of my competitors. Now I knew who I was up against.

"Were you satisfied with how that went?"

There was a small hesitation before he answered, "Yes, I— Yes, on the whole we were pretty much okay with it."

All right. Not a ringing endorsement of my rival. That was good.

I asked, "Would you give me an idea of what topics were covered?"

He ran through a short list from memory of the training points that had been discussed. I asked about exercises, follow-up, and a few other related things. As I talked, I began to mention how my program differed from what had been given to his sales force. I didn't make a big point of it, since I didn't want to seem as if I was giving my pitch all over. But I wanted to differentiate what I was offering from the service provided by the competition.

The prospect's answers became more detailed as we went on, and I was soon able to identify where he thought the main weaknesses of the training lay. When we'd vetted this topic to both our satisfaction, I moved things onto the next level.

"I can certainly see," I said, "that it's probably a bit early for another training session. But it's been my experience that the best thing is for salespeople to undergo this kind of training every 12 months. That way the lessons stay fresh. How about setting up a session with me nine months from now? I can cover . . ." I went into a discussion of the topics I'd deal with, including some that had been neglected by his previous vendor.

The long and short of it is that after some more discussion the prospect agreed to my proposal. Nine months later I had a training session with his salespeople. It went well, and I was able to set up a permanent gig at the company.

This is what I mean about changing the terms of the sale. I didn't sell what I'd intended—an immediate session with the sales force. However, by shifting from the present to the future I focused on getting something out of the call. And that's what really counts.

SOMETHING IS ALWAYS BETTER THAN NOTHING

This leads back to another one of my principles: it's always better to get something out of a sales call than nothing. Even if you won't see the benefits of that something for a while, it's still worthwhile if it can lead to a productive relationship. A salesperson who hears, "I don't need any at this time," and is thinking entirely about his commission will probably hang up and move on to the next call. His reasoning is that spending more time to try to get a future sale isn't cost-effective; the 10 or 15 minutes consumed by that would be better put to use on a prospect who might buy *now*.

In my opinion, this is a self-defeating approach. It's leaving money on the table, because a deferred sale now will become a real sale in the future. Of course, nobody likes waiting around for a ship to come in. But the important thing, in this case, is *developing a relationship with the prospect.*

IT'S ABOUT THE PEOPLE, STUPID!

This brings me to one of the most important, if obvious, truths about sales. Selling isn't about commissions, products, services, contracts, or any of that stuff. It's about people. You're selling to people, and you have to keep that in your mind at all times. Otherwise, you'll miss opportunities, and you'll never rise above the middle ranks of your chosen profession.

Selling is about developing relationships with people. Sometimes those relationships bear immediate fruit, and sometimes you have to cultivate them for a while before they start to ripen. You have to be patient.

I can't tell you how many young salespeople I've encountered who've boasted to me about making 20, 30, even 40 calls in a single day. My response is always, "Really? How much time are you spending on each call? How many questions are you asking? How well are you getting to know the people you're talking to?"

Selling is also about trust. You and the client are trying to solve a problem. The client trusts you to come up with a solution that will benefit him or her. And you can't trust someone you don't know. I'm not saying you have to wait until the client invites you over to his house for Sunday dinner. But your conversation has to develop in such a way that the client knows you have his or her interests at heart as well as the size of your commission.

If you rack up dozens and dozens of calls a day, through sheer volume you may get some impressive sales. But take a look at how many of those people buy from you again. How many of your clients are you able to follow up with? How strong is the bond you have with your repeat customers?

You have to find a sweet spot—the number of calls you can make during the day that will generate a significant volume of leads but will also give you the time during each call to develop a relationship with the person on the other end. Those relationships are what will generate sales, both today and in the future. Rushing through your call sheet as if it's some sort of contest just makes you look busy.

KEEP THE DISCUSSION GOING

Of course, sometimes the objection that the prospect doesn't need any now is just another way he has of trying to get you off the phone. After all, he's a busy man with people to see, spreadsheets to examine, and decisions to make. He doesn't have time for chit-chat with a salesperson.

There are two ways to approach this. One is the way I did in the phone call I described. I asked for a bit more of his time and kept on asking questions. One of the great advantages of questions is that people almost always feel obliged to answer them. And that keeps the discussion going and gives you more information you can use to develop a convincing pitch that will get the sale.

Another approach is to say, "I appreciate your candor, but I think we can still do some business together—maybe not today but sometime in the future. I'd like to discuss this more with you. Would next Monday at 10 a.m. be a good time for me to call again?" If you're going to do this, always be specific about when you want to talk, and make the proposal yourself. Don't wait for the prospect to do it. Ask, "Is there a good time for us to continue this?" and the answer will almost certainly be, "No, I'm completely tied up for the next month and a half."

During the phone call, keep the conversation on track, but don't be a fanatic about it. If the prospect wants to talk about something else for a bit, go with the flow. You'll pick up valuable information about her or his interests and concerns. The conversation doesn't always have to be about what you're selling. Sometimes it can veer off in unexpected directions that can give you insight into another possible sales opportunity. All of this comes back to the idea I've stressed elsewhere in this book: a sale is a conversation, not a presentation.

WHO MAKES THIS OBJECTION?

All four groups that I've discussed can and will make the objection about not needing anything from time to time. Some will be more sincere about it than others. Depending on whom you're speaking to, you have to be ready to deal with the objection in different ways.

1. *Dominant.* People who are part of this group are more likely to use this objection as a way of getting you off the phone. They don't like being tied up in sales calls for any length of time; they've got way too much to do. In this case, you're probably going to have to slow the conversation down. Ask for specific data—that's what this group loves to deal in. They don't want squishy opinions and feelings; just the facts, ma'am.

2. *Influence.* As networkers, these people like talking to you. In fact, you may have trouble getting off the call so you can move along with your day. They want to know everything about you—your family, your hobbies, the side on which you part your hair. When they raise this objection, it's almost certainly genuine, but you're unlikely to have trouble getting them to continue the conversation. Just make sure it doesn't go too far off track before you bring it back around to what you're selling and why they'll need it in the future.

3. *Steadiness.* Because these people don't like decisions, they're inclined to try to find ways of ending your pitch. This is a handy objection for such people precisely because of its vagueness. Your job in that case is to press for specificity. Why don't they need any at this time? When was the last time they used the product? How much of it do they have in stock? When do they anticipate needing to restock? What's the delivery time of their current vendor? Nail these people down and press for answers and you'll be able to pry open an opportunity.

4. *Conscientious.* Like Dominants, this group thrives on data. They want to keep on the straight and narrow—no side interests or discussions of vacation plans for them. So give them what they want. Ask about specifics, and then feed back to them a stream of information about what problem your product solves. Don't expect a big reaction, but you might get one when you show them why they'll need what you're selling in the future.

EVERYTHING YOU SAY IS TRUE

Hillary wrapped up her presentation with a flourish and sat back, feeling satisfied with herself. She'd hit all the points, pulled out the information from her PowerPoint, and finished with a nice flourish. Because she was a devotee of my school of sales presentation, she'd also made the pitch heavy with questions, letting the clients do most of the talking, keeping her questions open, and working to extract as much information as possible, making the session a real dialogue between two people trying to solve a mutual problem. Yes, she thought, this one's in the bag.

The client nodded thoughtfully. "That's it, then?" he asked.

"Yes, unless you've got any other questions?"

He nodded again and seemed to sink into a reverie. Something cold and hard began to knot in Hillary's chest. She waited, but the silence grew louder. She cleared her throat.

The client started slightly and looked at her. "Yes," he said. "Everything you say is true."

The silence began again, and then the client glanced at his watch and stood up. "Well," he said cheerfully, "thanks for coming in."

Five minutes later, Hillary was outside the door, her head spinning. As she sat in her car, reviewing the meeting, she kept asking herself, "Where did I go wrong?"

THE NONOBJECTION OBJECTION

Many years ago, I worked alongside a guy who had brought passive-aggressive behavior to the level of a fine art. The word *no* wasn't in his vocabulary—but somehow whenever he didn't want something to happen, it didn't happen. He could go into a meeting with a manager where the manager had a clear, written agenda, a specific set of takeaways to delegate, and a no-nonsense approach to getting things done. And somehow my coworker would emerge, sit down at his desk, and proceed to ignore whatever decisions had been taken by the meeting. He lived in his own little world, and it shouldn't come as a shock to you that six months later management politely asked him to find a different place to spend his time.

This objection is a good example of how some clients use passive-aggressive techniques to get rid of a sale they don't really want to take. It's one thing to make your pitch, encounter an objection, and overcome it head-on with the brilliance of your sales technique (to say nothing of mastering the contents of this book). It's another thing to come across a nonobjection objection. It's like putting your foot down firmly on the next step of a staircase only to find it isn't there. You want to argue, but there doesn't seem to be anything there to argue about. There's no basis to start asking questions, since the client implies that he has all the information he needs. And there's no basis for dialogue, because he's making clear that all he really wants is for you to be gone from his life.

So what can you do about it?

THE BASIS OF THIS OBJECTION

Start by understanding that even though it doesn't sound like one, this really *is* an objection. The client has avoided saying "no" directly, but *no* is what it is. You've walked away without a sale.

You then have to think about why the client doesn't want to say yes. Did you explain, clearly and with concrete examples, the advantages of the product or service you're selling? Did you focus on how it solves a problem for the company? Does the client understand the superior quality of what you're selling over the product or service of the competition? This can be a difficult list to go through, because you're groping in the dark at this point.

Once you've identified possible sources of opposition, you need to think through how to overcome them and retool your presentation with them in mind.

Now, I'm not suggesting that you do all this while you're standing there and the client is making noises at you that suggest he's got a very important meeting in three minutes and wants to thank you for your time and trouble. Instead, you need time to regroup. So find a closing line that *keeps the sale going*.

Client: I agree with everything you said. Thanks for coming.

Salesperson: I'm glad I touched on all the right points. I understand you've got a busy schedule. Would next Tuesday at three be a good time for us to pick this up again? I can rearrange my schedule to accommodate that.

Notice the subtle touch in the salesperson's technique—she's indicating that *she'll* take the trouble to rearrange *her* schedule for the benefit of the client. It makes it harder for him to say no to her without looking like a jerk. Follow this advice, and you'll avoid the problem of the salesperson I cited at the beginning of this chapter, who was out the door before she knew what hit her.

CLOSING TECHNIQUES

What did Hillary, the salesperson at the outset of this chapter, do wrong? After all, it seems as if she followed all the advice I give in my books. She asked questions, described benefits, kept the sale a dialogue rather than just a presentation. So what happened?

The biggest thing to know is that *she didn't close the sale.*

Closing techniques are tremendously important for sales-people—so much so that I've devoted an entire book to them: *Closing Techniques (That Really Work!)*. One of the important points I stress in the book is that your pitch has to end with a definite request to the client for a commitment. And that's what was missing at the end of Hillary's presentation. She got all of it right, but in the end, she didn't ask the client to buy. And that opened the door to this objection. So step one, obviously, is to revise the presentation to make sure it ends with a request to the client to buy.

In my book on closing techniques, I mention some ways to overcome objections such as "I don't have the time to discuss this more with you," or "I'll have to think about it." These are also nonobjection objections. One technique is to go back to a relatively innocuous part of your presentation and ask the client if you could have explained it better or suggest that perhaps you had a weakness in developing that point. That forces the client to do one of two things:

1. Either he will protest and tell you your presentation was great, in which case you can turn the conversation back to the issue of a buy from him.

2. He will agree (since it's always nice to feel superior to people). In that case, you can thank him for his advice and reexplain the point, once again bringing the conversation around to your request for a buy.

THE SECOND VISIT

Let's assume that, like Hillary, you've been ushered out of the office without making a sale, unable to break through the passive-aggressive veneer surrounding the client. But let's also assume that you've kept your cool and made a second appointment for a week later. Now you're ready and primed to overcome this objection and clinch the sale.

In the intervening time, you've improved your research on the company, looking for any more information that you can pile on the client as an additional reason to ink the deal. You've also spent some time thinking about the kind of person you're dealing with. As I'll make clear very shortly, within the four groups we've been considering several strongly incline toward passive-aggressive behavior and are thus likely to raise this objection.

Now you're ready to walk back through the door.

It's important that in this second sales call you take control of the meeting from the start. You're going to set the agenda and make sure it follows your rules. There's no point in running through every detail of what you said in the first sales call, but you should at least make sure the basic details are fresh in the client's mind.

Then turn to the crux of the meeting.

"Last time we spoke, you said you agreed with everything I said. That's great, because I think between us we've got a real opportunity here to improve the ABC Corporation's bottom line. What size order of our product did you have in mind?"

That's the crucial point—forcing the client out of passive-aggressive mode and into decision-making mode.

Of course, it's entirely possible that at this point the client will switch gears and come out with another objection. It's not only possible; it's likely, because now you're getting closer to the heart of the problem. The client will start to reveal, bit by bit, why she or he doesn't want to buy what you're selling. If that's the case, you can fall back on the extensive explanations you'll find elsewhere in this book of how to overcome each of these objections.

Second Meeting Techniques

These are some additional important techniques you need to master for this second meeting:

1. *Speak firmly and clearly.* A soft, hesitant voice puts you in the same situation as the client, who doesn't really want to discuss things. Pitch your voice to carry just beyond the client; don't shout, though. That will simply anger the client and get you tossed out of the office more quickly than you can imagine.

2. *Look directly at the client, but don't stare (there's a distinction).* Glaring at people makes them think you're angry with them. Looking steadily at them, with an occasional smile and motion of your head, will indicate your self-confidence as well as your interest in them.

3. *Use mirrored statements.* When the client says something, repeat it back in somewhat different words. For example:

Client: I think our most important concern is delivery of the product on time to make our major trade shows in June. That's been a concern in the past with other vendors.

Salesperson: I see. So you want to make sure you have the product in time for the major shows in June, right?

Client: Yes.

This method both makes for absolute clarity and increases the client's sense that you're actively involved in the conversation, listening and contributing.

4. *Be decisive and positive.* Passive-aggressive personalities thrive on doubt and hesitation. You don't have to oversell—a bad habit some salespeople fall into when they run into objections—but you *do* have to be confident in what you're selling. A decisive request for a commitment to buy will go a long way to overcoming this particular objection and forcing the passive-aggressive client to take a step backward.

WHO MAKES THIS OBJECTION?

As I said earlier, some personality types seem to breed passive-aggressive behavior. As a matter of fact, carefully used, it can be a useful sales technique in your arsenal. But that's a discussion for another time and place.

1. *Dominant.* As you might expect from the label, this group tends not to use the "everything you say is true" objection. They're much more willing to be in your face about what

they perceive as the problems or weaknesses of what you're selling. If you're speaking to a Dominant personality and this objection comes up, you should question whether it's just a tactical feint.

2. *Influence.* Part of the nature of passive aggression is to move conflict below the surface in an attempt to both hide and manipulate it. It's one of the things that make dealing with passive-aggressive people so difficult. They seem to want to avoid any open confrontation. It's this that makes passive aggression such a potent weapon in the hands of Influence people. After all, they want to like you, to avoid any appearance of conflict. So the easiest thing for them to do is to agree with you, congratulate you on your wonderful pitch, and quickly shoo you out the door. This is the group that will most often raise this objection.

3. *Steadiness.* There are times when members of this group will raise this objection. They don't like commitment, so they'll search for a way out, including agreeing with you. However, you're most likely to be able to sway them with a forceful, planned argument that requests a firm sales commitment.

4. *Conscientious.* This group's lack of enthusiasm for anything, including your sales presentation, makes it unlikely that they're actually going to tell you that they agree with you. On the other hand, they may find a variant of this objection and just sit on their hands until they run out the clock for the meeting and can safely get out of the room. Their skepticism, though, means that they're not necessarily averse to conflict. If they attempt to just wait you out, just reiterate your need for a definite agreement to buy and be prepared for a barrage of questions.

I'M WORRIED
ABOUT IT

A salesperson I know was working a room full of prospective clients. They were interested. He could feel it. The atmosphere in the room was swinging his way. In the back of his mind, he began to calculate his commission on this sale. He strolled back and forth in front of the screen where his carefully prepared PowerPoint slides were flashing in hypnotic succession. His mind was half on the presentation and half on the Aruba vacation he planned to take with the help of the bonus check it would bring in.

He finished with a flourish and said, in the confident tone of a man who knows he's left nothing to chance, "That's it, then! Any questions?"

There was silence for a few moments, and then the chief marketing officer of the company, the senior official in the room, stirred in his chair. He shook his head.

"I don't know," he said. "I'm worried about it."

Thoughts of the Caribbean vanished from the salesperson's mind. Now his hands were sweating, and his suit felt as if it were two sizes too small. He could feel small rivulets of moisture coursing along the back of his neck, but he didn't dare reach for a handkerchief to wipe them away.

He opened his mouth, and what came out was, "Uh . . ."

Well, you knew this story wasn't going to have a happy ending, didn't you?

GETTING AT THE TRUTH

The easiest sales objections to overcome are the most specific. If your client tells you, "I need 2,000 more units than you can deliver in this time frame," or "Your ETA to market is a week later than what works for us," you've identified a very specific problem. It's conceivable, of course, that you may not be able to resolve it, but at least you know what it is.

This objection, though, is different. It's so . . . nebulous. What does it mean, anyway? "I'm worried." Of course, he's worried. We're all worried! I'm worried every day when I get up . . . about how my business is going, about the state of the world, about whether the onions I had on my hamburger yesterday are going to give me gas. But I don't use that as a basis to kill a business deal that will directly benefit me. So what's he talking about?

The most common reaction to this kind of objection is the one displayed by our anonymous salesperson above. He doesn't have anything concrete to grab hold of, so he just shuts down. Even someone who keeps his cool might be tempted to break off the meeting at that point, or to get angry and start complaining about vague, undefined objections.

Enticing as these alternatives are, the most important thing, as I stressed in the previous chapter, is to keep the dialogue going. Keep in mind the fact that you haven't lost the sale yet. You haven't even really come close, although it might feel a bit like that. All that's happened is that someone's expressed a general, undirected reservation. Your job, should you choose to accept it, is to find out exactly what that reservation is. We've established that the client is worried. Taking that statement at face value, what's he worried about?

A SERIES OF QUESTIONS

If you're thinking that the thing to do here is ask questions, you're absolutely right, and you should give yourself a gold star for absorbing a lot of my sales methodology. But if you're thinking that the client is going to tell you what the problem is, you're being very naïve and should award yourself the Order of the Boot.

That the objection is phrased in this way—I'm worried—tells you one of two things is true. Either the client doesn't want the sale to go through but doesn't want to say why. or the client himself or herself doesn't really know what the objection is.

Let's take the first point first.

I Don't Want to Buy from You

If we assume that the client doesn't want to buy from us, we have to determine why. Is it the nature of what we're selling or is it something about us as a representative of a company? In either case, a direct question isn't likely to get much of an answer, since most clients are understandably reluctant to tell you flat out that they don't like you or what you're selling. (Some people will do that, of course. I once had a client say to me, "Steve, I just can't buy from someone who reminds me so much of a college professor I hated." In this instance, I was just stuck and couldn't think of a thing to say except, "So what grade did I give you?")

If a direct question won't work, sometimes you have to go through a list methodically, trying to eliminate the things that *aren't* making the client uncomfortable:

Salesperson: I see. Is what's worrying you connected with the product itself or with the way in which I presented it to you?

Client: I . . . don't know. I just feel there's a disconnect.

Salesperson: Would you perhaps tell me at what point in my presentation you began to feel this disconnect?

Client: Uh . . . no, I don't know.

Salesperson: Well, may I ask you this? Is it the product or the presentation?

Client: Oh, I think the product. Your pitch was fine.

Salesperson: Good to hear. I appreciate it. So there's a problem with the product. Are the features okay? Do they solve your problem?

Client: Yeah, I think so. It seems to do what you said it would.

Salesperson: Hmmm. Well, how about delivery date? Is that okay?

Client: To tell you the truth, that's kind of a problem for us. I was thinking we could really use delivery speeded up by three weeks.

Okay, finally we've started to get at the heart of the problem. Once you identify the real objection, you can solve it. At the same time, remember this may not be the client's only objection. It's entirely possible that there are several concerns rumbling around beneath the surface and you've got to determine which concern is the primary one and which ones are secondary.

It's You That's the Problem

If you yourself are the problem—if the client didn't like your pitch, your manner, the way you cut your hair, or if you reminded him of an old high school math teacher—your problem is both simpler and more complicated. This sort of objection usually happens at the very beginning of your relationship with the client, when you're still feeling out one another, trying to determine one another's styles and trustworthiness. As in any relationship, problems may arise, and this objection is one of the symptoms.

If this is really the situation, it's probably going to be very hard to get the client to actually talk about the issue. I remember a case many years ago in which a client raised this objection to me.

I talked to him for twenty-six and a half minutes, trying every trick I could think of to get him to tell me what he was worried about. He told me it wasn't the product's functions, delivery, cost, or service contract. It wasn't me. It wasn't anything about my company's reputation, location, or capacity. Oh, and it wasn't me. It wasn't the product's long-term viability or the state of his own company that was worrying him. And it wasn't *me*.

After the third or fourth time he repeated that it wasn't me, I finally got it. It *was* me—he just didn't want to say so. And no amount of probing on my part was going to get past that.

Under these circumstances, there were really only two courses open to me. I could have walked away from the sale, which would have been disappointing, since it was a large one that would have resulted in a significant commission.

Or I could do what I did: suggest a meeting in another week.

To that meeting, I brought another salesperson. She was about as different from me as you can get, starting with the fact that she was a *she*. I sat back and watched her make essentially the same pitch I'd made the previous week. And darned if this time the client didn't buy into it completely.

Naturally, my feelings were a bit hurt at first. But in thinking about it, I came to realize that sometimes the client himself doesn't know why he's worried. It's locked into his subconsciousness, and only a powerful blast of therapy is going to release it, which is something well beyond my capacity to provide. So the best thing I can do is to get out of the way of the sale. Let someone else make it. It's disappointing not to realize the commission, but better for me, for my company, and ultimately for the client that the sale go through.

WHO MAKES THIS OBJECTION?

Let's take a look at our different types and how they voice this objection that they're worried. It's a little simpler in this case, because we really only have to consider three groups.

1. **Dominant.** The Dominants aren't really a concern, as they don't usually object in these terms. It's not hard to see why: their personalities are outspoken. If they've got a problem either with you or with the product, of course they're going to tell you about it. In fact, a lot of the time they can't wait to do so. And their objections won't be voiced in the nebulous terms of this objection. Instead, if they don't like the price, they'll say, "I don't like the price." If they don't agree with the delivery schedule, they'll say, "Can't you speed up delivery?" Finally, if they don't like your presentation, they'll say, "You did a crappy job today. I'm not going to buy from someone who makes that sort of sloppy milquetoast

presentation. All this may be bruising to your ego, but at least it clarifies the situation.

The other three groups are each capable of making this objection, and you've got to find ways around them.

2. **Influence.** Since these people are all about connections and networking, they're inherently reluctant to do something that cuts off the conversation. From your point of view the problem may be that they want to talk *too* much. However, by the same token, they don't want to insult you, and that may well lead them to phrase their objection in this roundabout way. This is a group that you're going to have to prod and poke for awhile to get at what's bothering them.

3. **Steadiness.** Because they want you to like them, if the problem is your presentation, this group is very likely to voice their objection in this way. Remember that a key feature of this group is their reluctance to make a decision. Raising an objection in this vague, nondirectional form is a recipe for indecision. In the language of psychology, it's an avoidance mechanism. A useful way to approach this group is to return their overtures. If they want you to like them, make clear that you want to do just that. And that means expressing sympathy with them. Suggest that as their friend, you're deeply concerned with their worries. Handling the discussion this way is more likely to produce results than being confrontational or simply demanding that they explain themselves.

4. **Conscientious.** The lack of enthusiasm of the Conscientious group is always a big part of the problem in dealing

with them. In this case, they don't really want to appear enthusiastic about anything you've said, so this objection is a way of removing the energy from the room and putting you on the defensive. At the same time, their skeptical nature is capable of being wooed by logic, so a helpful approach is to take them, step by step, statistic by statistic, through the benefits the new product will bring to the company. For this group, come with a lot of facts and figures—don't rely on the charm of your personality to win the day.

I AM AN IDIOT

Contrary to the impression you may have formed reading these pages, I don't lose my temper easily. In truth, you can't be in sales as long as I have—for more than 30 years—and have a quick temper. There are too many situations in which you've got to breath very deeply, clench your hands until your fingernails drive into your palms, then smile and start the conversation over again.

Every now and then, though, something happens that sets me off. And as anyone who knows me will tell you, it's not a pretty sight.

Something along these lines happened to me several years ago. I'd made an appointment with a new lead, a company that was a bit outside my normal sphere of business. It was a medium-sized company with a line of products that were beginning to make something of a stir inside their industry. They were expanding their business, and they told me they wanted to increase the professionalism of their sales force. So I made the appointment with the CEO—I'll call him Mr. Smith—and set out for the call.

I advise salespeople to arrive at the site of a call a few minutes early to give yourself time to prepare—check that you've got everything for the presentation, use the facilities to check your hair, your breath, and so on. I showed up promptly at this company and, at 2:30 p.m. on the dot, introduced myself to the receptionist.

She gave me a blank look, as if I were selling spare parts for llamas. Then she busied herself with her computer for a few minutes and surfaced to say, "I'm sorry, Mr. Schiffman, but I don't seem to have you on Mr. Smith's schedule for today."

Mix-ups happen, of course, but it had been a long drive to get there and I'd missed lunch, so I wasn't in a good mood to begin with.

"Would you check again?" I asked. "I made the appointment with Mr. Smith personally last week."

The cloud behind her face seemed to clear. "Oh," she said. "That explains it. Mr. Smith doesn't always tell me when he schedules appointments."

It was on the tip of my tongue to say that must make her scheduling very complicated. However, at that point Mr. Smith himself came out of his office. He stared at me for a moment and clapped his hand to his forehead. "That's *right*!" he exclaimed. "Schiffman! We're supposed to talk today." He glanced at his watch. "Well . . ." He consulted his secretary for a few minutes in an undertone and then turned back to me. "I've got a meeting for 20 minutes right now. We can talk after that." Without waiting for an answer, he disappeared.

Internally steaming, I sat down. Thirty-eight minutes later he reappeared, looked at me as if he'd never seen me before in his life, and then clapped his hand to his head again. "Come on in," he told me.

We went into his office, which was jammed with folders and papers. He took a pile and moved it off a chair. "Sit here!" he commanded. "Now go ahead."

I've presented in some unusual situations, but this was high on the list. "You want me to present to you now?" I asked.

"Yeah. But make it quick. I've got a bunch of—" The buzz of the telephone interrupted him.

I did my best. I really did. During my pitch we were interrupted three more times by the telephone, once by a vice president who stuck his head in the door to ask a question, and finally by the secretary, who informed him that his 4 p.m. appointment was waiting (it was now 4:15).

He looked at me with a kind of sheepish smile. "I think we'll have to put the rest of this off until later," he said. "I'm not very organized."

Throughout this performance, I'd been feeling a pounding in my temples (possibly brought on by the fact that I still hadn't had anything to eat) and I could feel tiny beads of sweat popping up along my hairline. At his words, something snapped. I stood up.

"No!" I snarled. "You're not. And frankly you're not someone I want to do business with. Good luck!" And I walked out of his office forever.

THE DISORGANIZED INCOMPETENT

Not, I think you'll agree, my finest moment. But what do you do when you come face to face with a disorganized incompetent? Is it *really* your job to get him or her sufficiently organized to listen to your presentation? Is it *really* part of your brief as a salesperson to show him or her how to run the business?

Well, sometimes it is.

The first point to establish is whether the incompetence that's on display is genuine or assumed. After all, even though there are stupid and incompetent people who rise to great heights in business, companies often have a natural process of weeding them out. Someone who couldn't organize a two-car funeral is going to be exposed very quickly as an incompetent if he or she becomes part of the management team in an international business. And that person's superiors probably won't tolerate the kinds of mistakes that cost them money.

On the other hand, if someone wants to throw you off your stride or impede you from making a sale, a pretended display of disorganization can be an effective tactic.

The incompetence may also be a test. "Make me listen to you," the executive is saying. "Show me that your presentation can overcome the obstacles I'm throwing up at you."

A valuable clue as to whether the incompetence and disorganization are real or fake can be gleaned by looking around the office. If it's neat and efficient looking, and if it looks like the sort of place where serious business is transacted on a daily basis, it's far more likely that you're being subject to a ruse. However, as was the case in my experience above, if the office looks like a paper bomb went off in the middle of it, you may well be facing a genuine organizational disaster.

OVERCOMING THE OBJECTION

Let's consider first what to do if this objection is simply a tactic. What's behind it?

The client—or lead or prospect—wants above all to know how badly you want the sale. How much are you going to let get in the way of it? The client may also want to know how your product could overcome the kind of disorganization she's putting on display for you.

How do you cope with that?

1. *Propose an alternative.* When the client says, "I'm so sorry, I'm just a very disorganized person," smile and say, "Well, it certainly seems as if I've caught you on a busy day. Perhaps we should reschedule for a different time. I can set aside two hours next Tuesday between 2 and 4 p.m. Would that work for you? We can spend the first hour on the presentation itself and, if you'd care to invite in some of the sales force after that, I can demonstrate some exercises I put salespeople through in my training."

   An approach such as this is accommodating, organized, and specific. Effectively, you're showing the client that you can do the organizing for her.

2. *Step back.* Since the client wants to know how much you want the sale, take a small step backward. Say, "You appear to be very busy, and I'm afraid my time is also very valuable. Please contact me when you have a completely free hour for us to speak without interruptions." If you're right, and the client is merely testing you, she'll very quickly come up with a new appointment time—she may even tell her assistant, "Hold my calls for the next hour" and let you get down to it right then and there.

3. *Confront.* This is the riskiest approach, but it can be rewarding. When she says, "I'm just a very disorganized person," reply, "Yes, you seem to be. But what I'm selling can help you with that. And here's why." No one, of course, likes to be told she's disorganized, but if the client has been bluffing, she'll recognize that she's been called and will respond positively to your pitch for the virtues of your product.

WHAT IF THE INCOMPETENCE IS REAL?

But what if all the signs point to the fact that you're facing some-one who's genuinely disorganized, incompetent, or a bit stupid? Is it a dead end?

Not necessarily.

I've said repeatedly in this book that sales is all about help-ing the client to find solutions—and sometimes the client doesn't entirely understand the problem to which he needs a solution. In this case, part of the problem is his own weakness. So you'll have to do some quick thinking about how what you're selling can help overcome his disorganization.

The place to start, as usual, is with questions. These don't have to be abrupt or confrontational, although it may be tempting to start from there. You can ask something along the lines of, "I notice you seem very busy and a bit distracted today. I wonder if you would tell me if this is just a normal day for you?"

Assuming the answer's going to be yes, you should probe deeper. Ask about the causes of the tension and disruption. Ask about the structure of the organization. Ask about how the ex-ecutive thinks this is impacting the organization and his own career within it.

As you ask these questions, don't be judgmental in your re-sponses. At this stage you're simply gathering information, mean-while figuring out in your own mind how your product or service can contribute to a solution. Be patient—you'll probably have to exercise quite a lot of it as your meeting is interrupted and the executive gives rambling answers that don't go anywhere.

When you're ready, propose your solution. How can you help solve this issue? How will that benefit the company and him?

Specificity is your friend. People who are incompetents often don't have a strong grasp of detail, including schedules, deliverables, and takeaways. It's essential when you leave the meeting—particularly if you've not yet finished the discussion—that both of you have a clear set of understandings about what's going to happen next. In this sense, it *is* part of your responsibility to organize the unorganized. Goodness knows, if you leave it to the Mr. Smiths of this world, it won't get done.

It may also be possible and desirable to simply bypass the incompetent. You can always say something like, "I understand the difficulties you're having. Is there someone else it would be appropriate for me to speak to about this?" The incompetent manager may well be delighted to pass you off to someone else. (Disorganization for some people is a passive-aggressive strategy to avoid making decisions.)

If you choose this strategy, don't cut Mr. Smith out of your loop. This tactic is especially important if he refers you to someone lower on the chain of command. Mr. Smith may be disorganized, but he's not unaware of company protocol, and he'll appreciate you keeping him informed of the progress of your sale.

Finally—and after my opening example, it may strike you as funny that I should say this—try to keep your temper. Most of the time, even when confronted with the most disorganized and seemingly idiotic lead, it's possible when you come up against this objection to pull the sale out.

WHO MAKES THIS OBJECTION?

Any of our four groups are capable of being incompetent. However, when it comes to using this approach as a negotiating tactic, not all of them are comfortable using it.

1. *Dominant.* Because this group is anxious to dominate any discussion, they shy away from appearing stupid or out of

control. It's very unlikely that you'll see members of this group using this particular approach. As I've indicated elsewhere in this book, they're more likely to try to overwhelm you with their expertise.

2. *Influence.* Since they have no problem in confiding in you—members of this group want to be your best friend—it's quite possible they won't have any issue with telling you, "Oh, I'm just disorganized." However, if they make that statement, it's more apt to be true. It's not really in the nature of this group to try to deceive you.

3. *Steadiness.* This is the group most likely to make this objection—both as a tactic and as a genuine statement of their problem. Because they resist making decisions and dislike taking authority into their own hands, they often take refuge in their own inability. ("I'd *like* to buy what you're selling, but I'm just too darned confused to really decide just now!") However, they're also more apt to respond to your own strong expression of authority and organization.

4. *Conscientious.* These people, with their natural tendency toward skepticism combined with a strong desire for specific data, are often among the most organized people you'll meet. For this reason, it's unlikely any of them would use this objection unless it were a negotiating tactic.

I MAKE THE DECISIONS; THERE IS NO ONE ELSE TO SEE

24

There I was, sitting at the edge of my chair, my PowerPoint slides neatly stacked in front of me. My tie felt as if it was too tight, and my palms were sweaty. My eyes were hot and stinging, and there was a tightness in my chest.

In short, I was mad as hell.

The vice president of operations sat across from me, his legs crossed, arms folded over one another. The very picture of rejection.

I took a deep breath and tried again. "I understand what you're saying," I said, "but just hear me out. I . . ."

The VP pushed his chair back from the table. "There's no point in continuing this," he snapped. "I said no, and I mean no."

"Well," I said, making an effort to keep calm, "I've offered this training seminar to your company a number of times before, and it's always worked. Perhaps you and I could consult with the CEO . . ."

The VP slammed his hand down on the table explosively. "*No!*" he almost shouted. "*I* make the decisions about this! *I* decide what training the sales force need! And I say *no!*"

That did it. I stood up and slammed my presentation into my briefcase. Striding to the door, I turned and snarled, "Fine! I'll just cross you guys off my list. Good luck getting a trained sales force!" And I banged the door shut for emphasis.

I've mentioned a number of these scenarios now, and some of you are going to get the idea that I fly off the handle at a moment's notice when I run into an objection. That isn't the case; I'm afraid you'll have to take my word for it.

I don't object to getting angry occasionally; it can be a very useful technique in sales and negotiations. But I recommend a controlled anger, not an emotional outburst of the type that I threw. In truth, the guy got my goat because I knew he was wrong. And he knew I knew. He *didn't* always make those decisions, and if we'd gone to the CEO, I'm pretty sure I could have sold him my seminar, not least because I could point to solid, practical results for his own firm since they'd started doing it.

The VP was new to the company and obviously intent on throwing his weight around a bit. I should have recognized that, fallen back, and regrouped. Sales can be a lot like war. Sometimes in battle a strategic retreat is the best course possible, and that was the case here. Sadly, I let my emotions get the best of me. The VP reported to the CEO that I'd barged out of the meeting, and that ended any chance I had of selling to that company.

THERE'S ALWAYS SOMEONE ELSE

What *should* I have done?

To answer that, you have to keep in mind that except for very small companies, most of the time you will not be selling to the person in charge. The bigger the company, of course, the lower on the totem pole will be the person you're selling to.

Before you walk into the room, when you're doing your research on the company, determine where in the pecking order the person to whom you're going to be talking falls. See if you can determine from that person's title how much authority he or she actually has. The most immediate question is, does that person have the power to buy what you're selling? The second question is, if he or she doesn't have that authority, who does?

Make a company organization chart, filling in as many names as you can. Who reports to whom? Who is in charge of which areas? Don't worry if many of these areas have nothing to do with you and what you're selling—at this point you're accumulating information about the company as a whole. These days you can find a lot of this information online at sites such as www.hoovers.com.

After your meeting with the client, add to the information on the organization chart any further data that you've gleaned from your visit. Make it as comprehensive as possible, with notes on it indicating possible future contacts. Where you can, include contact information: phone numbers, e-mail addresses, and so on.

When someone raises the objection about making all the decisions, don't fight it openly. Instead, fall back and consolidate your forces. Smile politely, shake hands, and leave the room. You may be furious inside, but there's no reason to show it. Instead, go back to your organization chart. Ask yourself who else in the organization you can approach.

THE GATEKEEPERS

As you proceed up the ladder of the company, looking for new prospects, you'll quickly run into a group of people whose job it is to stop you from talking to their bosses. These are the people I call gatekeepers: secretaries, assistants, and so on. When you call, they'll block your contact and, in all likelihood, refer you back down to where you came from.

There are a couple of ways to get past these people. I discuss some of them in my book *Cold Calling Techniques (That Really Work!)*.

Phone Calls

When a gatekeeper intercepts your call, she or he will want to know your name and your business. You must give this information honestly; no one is going to deal with you if you lie about something like that. At the same time, you can take the initiative; for instance:

Gatekeeper: Mr. Bigshot's office.

Salesperson: Hi, this is Ms. Smith from the XYZ Company. I'd like to speak to Mr. Bigshot, please.

Gatekeeper: May I ask what this is in reference to?

Salesperson: I have a product I'd like to discuss with him. Would you connect me to him, please?

Gatekeeper: One moment, please.

Much of your success here will depend on having a strong, confident tone. You have to assume that of *course* Mr. Bigshot would want to talk to you.

It's also possible to use the name of the objector. For instance, you can say, "I'd like to talk to Mr. Bigshot with reference to a conversation I had recently with Ms. Brown in Purchasing." A

name will lend authority to you and make Mr. Bigshot more inclined to talk to you, since he (and his assistant) now know that
you've already spoken to someone in the company.

GET THEIR ATTENTION

When you're connected to Mr. Bigshot, always address him by
name and acknowledge his title. Explain quickly and clearly what
you're selling. Remember that the higher you go in the company
the less time executives have to listen to you.

Do *not* spend your time complaining about the objector. Mr.
Bigshot's instinct will be to defend his employee. In any case,
it's possible that the objector has already passed the word up to
Mr. Bigshot about his rejection of your pitch. Your job now is to
make that pitch as compelling and straightforward as possible.
So don't waste time trying to get to know Mr. Bigshot, asking
about his kids, or wondering how his day is going. He doesn't
have time for that, and neither do you.

When you've made your pitch, one of four things will happen:

1. Mr. Bigshot will agree to the sale. This is the most desired outcome, but in some ways it's the least likely. After all, this isn't
   a decision that's made lightly. Mr. Bigshot didn't get where
   he's at in the company by agreeing to proposals without a lot
   of data and consideration.

2. Mr. Bigshot will confirm the objector and tell you he's not interested. Don't spend a lot of time arguing, which isn't likely
   to get you anywhere. Instead, take the opportunity to try to
   establish a permanent lead. Say something like, "Well, I appreciate your difficulty, and I respect your decision. But I have
   some other products that will be coming on the market in

another month. I'd like to discuss these with you when, perhaps, you have more time at your disposal. Would this Wednesday at 2 p.m. be a good time for us to continue this conversation?" The proposed time isn't important; at this point you'll probably be sent back to the gatekeeper, who is in charge of Mr. Bigshot's schedule. But that's fine. As long as you're going to talk again and you have a definite date, the call has accomplished something.

3. Mr. Bigshot will refer you back to the objector. This is the outcome you want the least, since it means you're back where you started. But again, don't spend time arguing. Instead, sit down with your organization chart and see if you can find another angle of attack.

4. Mr. Bigshot will ask for more information. This request is great, since you're more than happy to supply it. If he has time, you can continue the discussion right now, but if, as is likely, he's got a dozen other matters pending on his desk, set up a time for another meeting to present the full version of your pitch.

THE POWER OF VOICE MAIL

When you call, it's quite possible that the gatekeeper, rather than switching you directly to Mr. Bigshot, will connect you to his voice mail. A lot of salespeople suffer from an inability to leave compelling voice-mail messages. I discuss this fully in *Cold Calling Techniques (That Really Work!)*. What follows is the shortened version.

Leave your name, the name of your company, and a contact phone number. Again, you *must* be honest. Neglecting to leave the name of your company will just anger Mr. Bigshot when, and if, he calls you back.

One useful technique is to reference the name of the objector. For instance:

"Hi, this is Steve Schiffman from DEI calling. My phone number is 555-1212. I'm calling in reference to Jane Brown. I'd like to set up an appointment to see you at your earliest convenience." There's nothing dishonest about this; you *are* calling about Jane Brown and about her objection to your pitch. You just don't need to spell all that out in detail.

The object of these phone calls and phone messages is to get a face-to-face appointment with Mr. Bigshot. Once you do that, you can make your detailed pitch of your product and service. But remember, there's *always* someone else to talk to.

WHO MAKES THIS OBJECTION?

Because this "*I* make the decisions!" objection is rather aggressive and in-your-face, several of the groups that we've been considering are more likely to raise it than others.

1. *Dominants.* Their very nature pushes them toward this objection. They want to be the ones who make all the big decisions in the company, whether they have the authority or not. They're determined that no one is going to push them around, and once they say no to you, that's it. There's really no point in arguing the matter with them. If they say no, smile, leave, and start plotting your assault on the upper echelons of the company.

2. *Influence.* Because of the interconnected nature of these people, they're unlikely to raise this objection. In fact, they

like to have contacts on all levels of the company, as well as outside it. In this role, they're enormously helpful in assisting you to understand the nature and structure of the company and often in introducing you to key people in the organization. Take full advantage of this. These are the kinds of people whom you can call up and say, "Listen, I'm trying to get hold of the CFO but I don't know her phone number. Would you help me out?"

3. *Steadiness.* Because of their dislike of making a decision, members of this group are relatively unlikely to make this objection. In fact, often they'd rather that you talked to someone else. Their preference is for executing rather than deciding, so they're likely to help you in your search for someone who can make the decision to buy and who is willing to do so.

4. *Conscientious.* Like the Dominants, this group will often make this objection. They don't like having their authority questioned. They won't be aggressive about it (the way that Dominants will), but they're not going to help you either. Leave, without slamming doors, and go back to your organization chart for your next move.

NO!

25

One of the things I love about my job, training salespeople, is the immensely creative ways they have of going about what they do. Despite my many years of work in this field, I don't think a single year has gone by without someone, somewhere, coming up with a novel solution to working around a sales objection. Whether it's over it, under it, around it, or through it, salespeople, once they really get a grip and start to think about things, will find a way to make the sale.

Well, almost.

My own experience in this regard has been instructional. One day about 15 years ago I went through a pitch to a company. It had never had training for its sales force before, and it was pretty clear from the outset that the executives I was pitching to didn't see why they should start now. Right from the moment I started talking, the objections began to come fast and furious:

- "It's too expensive."

- "We've never done it before."

- "Our salespeople do fine the way they are."

- "This would break down our customer relations."

- "You don't understand this company's culture."

And so on. I felt like the proverbial Dutch boy, trying to stem the leaks in a dike that was moving fast toward collapse. But the longer I talked and the longer I worked at it, the more I felt as if I was making progress.

But I had one eye on the CEO, who was sitting at the far end of the table, not saying much. He was letting his VPs do most of the heavy lifting in the discussion and seemed to be taking it all in. I figured that because he wasn't talking, he was probably seeing how well I was handling the various objections flying at me. Finally, at the end of a very long hour, he leaned forward.

"Steve," he said, "I want to thank you for coming in here today. You've done an impressive job, and I know we've put you through the wringer. I appreciate what you're offering, but I have to tell you that we're just not ready to buy your service at this time."

Almost automatically, I started to reach for my responses. "Well," I said, "I think perhaps we could continue this discussion next week when you've had a chance to understand the benefits of . . ."

He shook his head. "No, I don't think that's necessary."

I countered. "Suppose I leave some material and you can talk about how much my program can mean in dollars and cents to your company."

He shook his head again and stood up. "I appreciate your time, Steve."

I tried one more time. "Perhaps if we discussed a smaller, less expensive pilot training program . . ."

"Steve!" He wasn't smiling anymore. He looked annoyed, and the VPs around the table had shrunk back into themselves.

"I thought I made myself clear. We're *not* going to buy what you're selling. Just leave it there."

WHEN NO MEANS NO

At universities in MBA programs, classes in sales are in the business school. Sometimes I think that's a mistake. They should be moved to the psychology department instead, because that's really what we focus on in this business—trying to understand, to get inside the heads of those whom we're selling to. As I've made clear throughout this book, I think it's useful and important to analyze your audience and figure out what motivates them. You don't have to use the four types I've provided—although I think they're extremely helpful—but you do need to spend a lot of time understanding why people buy and why they're more or less likely to buy from you. And you need to be acutely sensitive to what I would call atmospheric shifts in meetings, when the weather can change in a heartbeat from sunny to stormy to hurricane expected momentarily.

In the example I just gave, I failed to anticipate this. Most important, I didn't see that sometimes no just means no. The longer I tried to change the CEO's objection, the less likely it became that I was going to make a sale.

So what's the option in this case? Full-out retreat?

No, absolutely not. But the first step is to recognize when you're confronted by an objection that you can't overcome. Here are some guidelines to doing so:

1. A firm, unbreakable objection is likely to come from the top echelons of a company. As I indicated in Chapter 24, someone

lower down on the totem pole telling you no doesn't have the same force as the CEO or CFO saying it. When the head of the company says no, she or he is likely to mean it.

2. Watch for body language. Someone who wants to impress you with the forcefulness of his or her objection is likely to stand (since standing is a dominant position) and lean forward. They will look directly at you and speak clearly and firmly.

3. To cut off possible avenues of attack on your part, they'll often anticipate them in advance; for example: "I realize you're offering us a great deal from the standpoint of price, but we're not interested."

4. The objection will be presented as an absolute. Not "We can't consider your product at this time" or "We don't anticipate a need in the immediate future for what you're selling" but "No. Not now. Not in the future. Just no."

WHAT SHOULD YOU DO?

The worst thing you can do when the objection comes in this form is to try to change the objector's mind. That tactic isn't going to work, and it's going to make things get very unpleasant very quickly. You may not get chased out of the office at the business end of a shotgun, but the end result will be very much the same. Instead, you have got to think of what the objector wants from you.

First, he clearly doesn't want to continue the conversation. That's why he's ending it. Read the signs, and be willing to exit quickly and without a fuss.

He wants you to respect his ability and authority to make this decision. You can verbally acknowledge this in a simple, straightforward way as you're packing up your briefcase: "Well, you're the boss, and while I'm disappointed, you're the one who gets paid to make those kinds of decisions." Any implication that you'll attempt to undermine his authority will get you booted from the building in short order.

Finally, he wants the termination of the sale to be as stress-free as possible under the circumstances. Keep that in mind. Slamming your presentation papers into your briefcase, darting glares at him under lowered eyebrows, or muttering imprecations under your breath isn't going to do anything but ensure that you'll be persona non grata for the foreseeable future.

And that is the key to the whole thing: there's always the future. After all, a number of things might happen:

- The CEO might lose his job or move on to another company, leaving another opportunity for you to sell to this firm.

- Evolution of the industry might force him to reconsider and better understand the value of what you're selling.

- He might change his mind after thinking about it for a while. Even though he's said no, that doesn't mean your presentation hasn't kicked over a few things in his mind.

- Others who listened to your presentation might persuade him that he was mistaken in saying no.

The point is that just because he's said no and meant it, you shouldn't give up.

THE VALUE OF A GOOD RETREAT

Retreat in warfare is one of the hardest things to do and do well. Napoleon Bonaparte found that out when he attacked Russia in 1812. Having captured Moscow (and accidentally set it on fire), under the pressures of the oncoming Russian winter he began a long retreat back through Prussia and ultimately to France. The retreat was a disaster. Without adequate clothing to protect them from subzero temperatures, thousands of Napoleon's soldiers froze to death. Food was inadequate and horses died by the score, which meant that growing numbers of soldiers tramped the long miles on feet that bled; they were clad in nothing more than filthy rags. The Grande Armée literally melted away. Napoleon was forced to surrender to allied forces and began his exile on the faraway island of Elba.

History is full of equally disastrous retreats, some of which have spelled the downfall of empires. But a good retreat is another matter. In 1940, when the British Expeditionary Force was trapped by invading German armies, the British government, in a supreme effort, evacuated more than 338,000 troops and more than 40,000 vehicles from the port of Dunkirk. The events of Dunkirk were testimony to the organization and strength of will of the new British government led by Winston Churchill.

Just as the British saved their army to fight—and eventually conquer—another day, so you've got to be willing to retreat in the face of a forceful, definite, and firm objection in order that you can better overcome it in the future.

The most important tool you have when faced with this objection is your business card. It's small but powerful. Because it's a way of keeping your name in the system, of letting the company executives know that even though they haven't bought what you're selling, you're not giving up on them.

Churchill said, "Wars are not won by evacuations." That's true. Your carefully executed retreat, respecting the objecting executive and at the same time preserving your small foothold inside the company, can place you in an admirable position to step forward when circumstances change, when you're ready to sell, and they're ready to buy.

WHO MAKES THIS OBJECTION?

All four groups can and will make this "No!" objection. You can, though, discern some differences in the way they'll voice it.

1. *Dominant.* Members of this group won't have any hesitation in telling you that no means no. They're also the most likely to get angry if you keep trying to push back in the face of this objection. Since this group, as I've noted through the book, doesn't hesitate to voice its opinions in a forceful way, you may have some trouble seeing when their objections are set in stone. But be sure to watch carefully for that moment when you run into an immovable obstacle; then step back cautiously from it.

2. *Influence.* Members of the Influence group don't want to lose touch with you, and their very friendliness can seduce you into thinking that just because they've said no they don't really mean it. Don't fall into this trap! Getting on the wrong side of this group can be disastrous. Since they're networkers, they're adept at spreading the word widely, and a reputation with them as an obnoxious personality can quickly be spread far and wide.

3. *Steadiness.* Even though this group dislikes making decisions, they like even less having them questioned, because it requires them to go through the process of making them again. So if a member of this group says no, it's probably time for a quick retreat and consolidation.

4. *Conscientious.* Members of this group may not show much enthusiasm, but they know what they like—and what they don't like. They focus on facts and hard data, and once they've absorbed it, they don't appreciate any suggestion that their decision has been hasty or ill informed.

But with all four groups, remember—no may mean no, but it never means good-bye.

INDEX